D0562877

bor Seki

no Seki-kun

5

Takuma Morishige

Schedule			
56th Period ③	57th Period ⑬	58th Period ㉓	59th Period ㉝
60th Period ㊸	61st Period ⑥⑤	62nd Period ⑦⑤	63rd Period ⑧⑤
64th Period ⑨⑤	65th Period ⑩⑦	66th Period ⑫⑦	67th Period ⑭⑦
68th Period ⑮⑦	Bonus ① ⑯⑦	Bonus ② ⑰①	

My Neighbor Seki

5

* THIS IS A WORK OF FICTION. NAMES, CHARACTERS, PLACES AND INCIDENTS ARE PRODUCTS OF THE AUTHOR'S IMAGINATION OR USED FICTITIOUSLY. ANY RESEMBLANCE TO ACTUAL EVENTS OR LOCALES OR PERSONS, LIVING OR DEAD, IS ENTIRELY COINCIDENTAL.

Cranbury Public Library
23 North Main St., Cranbury, NJ 08512
(609) 655-0555 f: (609) 655-2858
www.CranburyPublicLibrary.org

My Neighbor Seki, volume 5

Tonari no Seki-kun

A Vertical Comics Edition

Translation: Mari Morimoto
Production: Risa Cho
Anthony Quintessenza

© Takuma Morishige 2014
Edited by MEDIA FACTORY
First published in Japan in 2014 by KADOKAWA CORPORATION, Tokyo.
English translation rights reserved by Vertical, Inc.
Under the license from KADOKAWA CORPORATION, Tokyo.

Translation provided by Vertical Comics, 2015
Published by Vertical Comics, an imprint of Vertical, Inc., New York

Originally published in Japanese as *Tonari no Seki-kun 5* by MEDIA FACTORY.
Tonari no Seki-kun first serialized in *Gekkan Comic Flapper*, MEDIA FACTORY, 2010-

This is a work of fiction.

ISBN: 978-1-941220-89-4

Manufactured in the United States of America

First Edition

Second Printing

Vertical, Inc.
451 Park Avenue South
7th Floor
New York, NY 10016
www.vertical-comics.com

Vertical books are distributed through Penguin-Random House Publisher Services.

56th Period

...

THIS POLI-CY...
AND SO,

HE'S PLAYING LIKE A KID DURING CLASS AGAIN.
A DIRT BALL ...

コロ
ROLL
コロ
ROLL

...
キュッ
SQK
キュッ
SQK

NOT THAT I RECALL WHY I WAS SO OBSESSED.
WELL, I MADE MY SHARE WHEN I WAS YOUNG.

AH!
TIMEL
コロ

FSH
すっ
HE PUT IT ON A BAMBOO LEAF! NOW IT REALLY LOOKS LIKE A DUMPLING!
Even that?

WHAT A SMOOTH SURFACE!
IT LOOKS LIKE A REAL RED BEAN PASTE DUMPLING!
Leave it to Seki!

ROLL
コロ
ROLL
コロ
ROLL
コロ
HM ?

HE'S ON TO THE NEXT ONE.
AN ENDLESS PROJECT ...
PRESS-
ギュ

ハッ
AH!

IS IT MY IMAGI-NA-TION?
THE COLOR SEEMS DIFFERENT FROM THE FIRST ONE...

HE'S SWITCHING DIRT TYPES WITH EACH DUMPLING ?!
DIRT !!

ABOUT DIRT DUMP-LINGS?
WHY'S HE BEING SO FUSSY

DID HE COLLECT THEM FROM SEPARATE SPOTS TO GET DIFFERENT COLORS?
THERE'S BLACK, OCHER, AND GREENISH, AS IF MIXED WITH MOSS.

WHOA!

ギュッ
SQK
ギュッ
SQK

MUGWORT!
ROASTED SOYBEAN FLOUR!
RED BEAN PASTE!
HE HAS A COMPLETE TRICOLOR SET!!

...
THOUGH I THINK HE SHOULD'VE JUST MADE REAL DUMP-LINGS.

Looks yummy.
SUCH QUALITY WITH JUST DIRT.
SEKI'S WORK IS ALWAYS IMPRESSIVE, BUT IT'S EXTRA REFINED TODAY.

grrowl

IT'S 4TH PERIOD, JUST BEFORE LUNCH.
NOT THAT I CAN BLAME HIM.

ARE THE HYPER-REALISTIC DUMPLINGS WHETTING HIS APPE-TITE?!
IS THAT SEKI'S STOMACH ?!
ぎゅるるるる
GRROOWL

I BET THE WHOLE CLASS IS STARVING.
IN FACT, SEKI'S LIKELY NOT THE ONLY ONE.

IT'S A SCHEDULE THAT'D CAUSE MAXIMUM HUNGER.
AND 3RD PERIOD WAS P.E.
WE HAD A SCHOOL ASSEMBLY THIS MORNING,

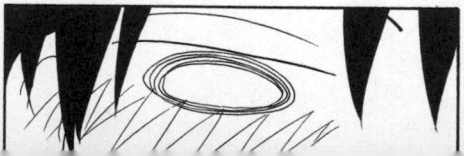

AHH
あーん
HM ?!
SEKI?!
はっ
GASP
SHFF
HAS HE GONE MAD FROM HUNGER ?!
SEKI REALLY WAS ABOUT TO EAT THAT DIRT DUMP-LING!
RUMBLE
GROWL
ぐーぎゅるる
...
SHAKE
ぶんっ
ぶん
SHAKE
OH NO, NOT AGAIN.

SCARF
HE'S EATING HIS LUNCH!!
SCARF
SCARF

RUSTLE

AH!

!
WAFT

GOOFING TAKES PRECEDENCE OVER ALL.
IS HE TIDING HIMSELF OVER TO AVOID EATING HIS DIRT DUMPLINGS?
How can you eat meatballs right now?
MNCH-
MNCH

growl

SEKI, YOU IDIOT! BE CONSIDERATE OF THE PEOPLE AROUND YOU!
THE SMELL OF HIS LUNCH IS GONNA MAKE MY STOMACH GROWL!

THE HUNGER DAMAGE IS SPREADING!!
grrr
growl
rrumble

CAN HE GET AWAY WITH SUCH A DEVIL-MAY-CARE LIFE-STYLE?!
AH, THERE HE GOES AGAIN!
ROLL
ROLL
ROLL
ROLL
ROLL

THIS IS A SERIOUS CRIME, SEKI!
YOU'RE THE ONLY ONE WITH A SATISFIED LOOK!
URP

HUH ?!

WHAT'S GOING ON...?
OR LIKE SOME-THING SEKI MADE HIMSELF.

WEIRD!
IT DOESN'T LOOK TASTY AT ALL !!

DID HIS HUNGER ADD THE SPICE NEEDED TO MAKE IT LOOK SO TASTY?
WAS IT BECAUSE HE WAS HUNGRY?
Huh
SOK
ギュッ
SOK
ギュッ

WHAM
HE SMASHED IT!

...
It's PUNISHMENT FOR EATING YOUR LUNCH EARLY.
SEKI'S ANGUISH CONTIN-UED UNTIL THE CLASS BELL RANG.
ぐしゃっ
CRUSH

SEKI'S ENTERED AN UNPREC-EDENTED SLUMP?!
NOW THAT HIS APPETITE'S SATED, THAT DIVINE QUALITY IS NO LONGER REPRODUC-IBLE?!

57th Period

KLAK
カチャ
KLAK
カチャ

FROM SAID EXPERI-MENT...

SHOULD YOU REALLY PLAY AROUND SO OBVIOUSLY IN THIS ROOM?
ARE YOU SURE?

SHOGI?!

LET'S PLAY SHOGI JENGA!
KLATTER
KLATTER

SEE? YOU'VE BEEN FOUND OUT BY UZAWA!!
KACHAK
OOH, SHOGI!
NICE! YOU BROUGHT GOOD STUFF!

HE SHOULD PAY ATTENTION IN THIS CLASS AT LEAST.
BUT SEKI WON'T LEARN.

ARGH...
AS OVER-BEARING AS USUAL.
GOT ONE, SO IT'S MY TURN AGAIN!

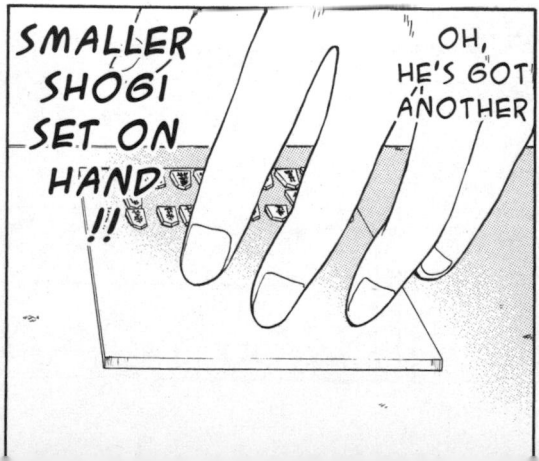
SMALLER SHOGI SET ON HAND!!
OH, HE'S GOT ANOTHER

SNEAK
HM?

TODAY SEKI IS A SCHEMER !!
HE'S NOT LETTING UZAWA JERK HIM AROUND ANY-MORE!
WAS HIS GOOFING OFF EARLIER JUST AN ACT TO HOOK UZAWA?
HAD HE FIGURED THAT UZAWA WOULD TAKE OVER THE OTHER ONE?!
The board is the same color as the desk.
SFF
SFF
HOW DOES HE PLAN TO PLAY WITHOUT OPPO-NENTS?
HM? THIS SET ONLY HAS HALF THE PIECES.
I DON'T GET IT. WHAT'S THE POINT ...?
HE'S JUST LINING UP AND MOVING THEM AROUND?
AH!
SFF
SFF

HE'S MAKING THE PIECES UNDERGO MILITARY DRILLS ?!
ZSH
ZSH
NO WAY! IS THIS A TRAIN-ING EXER-CISE ?!

OH, BUT HE IS ENJOYING HIMSELF.
I GUESS IT'S OKAY, THEN.

NO, NO, THAT'S MEANINGLESS.
IT CAN'T BE ANY FUN JUST ARRANGING AND SHUFFLING THEM ABOUT WITHOUT A MATCH.

OOH, A GOLD GEN-ERAL!
Yay!

DOESN'T SEEM LIKE WE'RE IN CLASS.
BUT GEEZ, THIS PANORAMA BEFORE ME...

WHSH
KNOCK THE REST OUT WITH A GOLD MISSILE!
AMASH
FWAP

Bishop

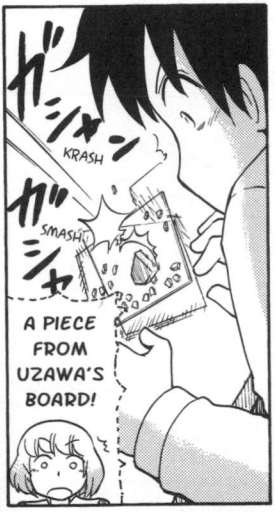
KRASH
SMASH
A PIECE FROM UZAWA'S BOARD!

JUST CAME HURTLING OUT OF THE SKY!!

A GINOR-MOUS ENEMY!

HE CAN'T JUST IGNORE AND CLEAR OUT THAT PIECE, EVEN THOUGH HIS ARCH-NEMESIS UZAWA CAUSED IT!
GIVEN PAST TRENDS, SEKI'S GAMES OCCUR IN REAL TIME! UNFORESEEN CIRCUM-STANCES ARE HANDLED LIKE DEVELOP-MENTS.

SKAK
スチャ

IT'LL BE WORTH WATCHING HOW HE HANDLES A BIGGER OPPO-NENT.
YOU KNOW, SEKI USUALLY SIDES WITH THOSE WHO BULLY THE WEAK.
heh heh

SKAF
OH!
It moved ?!

DID YOU DO SOME-THING, SEKI?
IT LOOKS THE SAME AS BEFORE, BUT...
?

サッ SAF
サッ SAF

HE'S TILTING THE WHOLE BOARD TO DISLODGE THE GIANT BISHOP?!
WHAT A MAGNIFICENT TRAP!!
OVER THERE!!
は,
AH!
BUT WON'T THE KING AND OTHER PIECES ALSO SLIDE OFF?
カタ
KTAK
カタ
KTAK
DX Chogokin
IF SO, IT'S A GREAT STRATEGY THAT TAKES ADVANTAGE OF THE TERRAIN!
THE BIGGER ONE IS MADE OF WOOD!
COULD THE SMALLER BOARD BE METAL AND ITS PIECES MAGNETS?!

AH!
KLUNK
SLIDE
ガラ
ゴン

グラ
STAGGER
グラ
STAGGER
OH, NOO!

THEY'RE ALL SMALL BUT WORTHY!
THIS IS A WIN FOR TEAM-WORK!

THEY FELLED HIM!!

I'VE REVISED MY OPINION OF YOU!
YOU POSSESS AN IN-DOMI-TABLE SPIRIT!
GOOD JOB TO YOU, TOO, SEKI!

I'M DONE, I'M BORED NOW.
KLATTER
ガラ
ガラ
KLATTER
飛車

KLAK
KLAK
カチャ
カチャ

...

SEKI WAS UTTERLY DEFEATED AGAIN.
HE'S TOTALLY LOST THE WILL TO FIGHT.
HE FLED TO A DIFFERENT SEAT!
Baah

こそこそ
こそこそ

RUMMAGE
ゴソゴソ

• 58th Period •
SKRITCH
カリ
SKRITCH
カリ
SKRITCH
カリ

どちゃっ
THMP

カタッ
KTAK

SKFF
ゴソ
SKFF
ゴソ

AH!
KCHAK
カチャッ

WHAT THE HECK IS HE TRYING TO DO?
How'd he fit them in his bag?
I WAS GONNA IGNORE HIM, BUT THERE'S SO MUCH STUFF TODAY!

THEY USED TO SELL THOSE IN TOY STORES.
THAT TAKES ME BACK!

IS THAT A ROBOT ARM?
KASHIK カシュ
KASHIK カシュッ

パッ
KLOP

BUT DOES HE REALLY NEED TO USE A ROBOT ARM FOR THAT...?
I SEE, HE'S GONNA PLAY BY STACKING THOSE MINI BINS, EHUH.

TMP トニッ

SPOP カポッ

KLAK カタ

HE'S JUST SEALING AND STACKING THEM WITH THE ROBOT ARM?
ARE THEY TUPPERWARE HIS MOM USES IN THE KITCHEN?
THEY LOOK LIKE ORDINARY PLASTIC CONTAINERS.
HUSSH
HUH? THAT'S IT?
スッ
SHFF
OH, HE'S FINISHED ANOTHER SET ALREADY!
THE EXACT SAME THING ?!
IT DOESN'T SEEM LIKE HE'S GONNA DO ANYTHING SPECIAL.
Hm?
はっ
AH!
カタン
KLAK
カパッ
SPOP
コトン
TMP
WHAT'S HIS GOAL?!

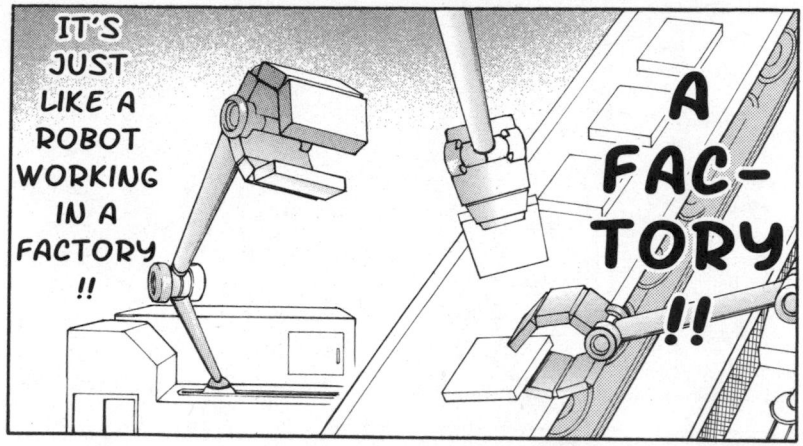
IT'S JUST LIKE A ROBOT WORKING IN A FACTORY !!
A FAC-TORY !!

BEING JUST MA-CHINES.
CLEVER ROBOTS THAT ALMOST SEEM ALIVE DESPITE
TRUE, SEEING ROBOTS IN ACTION ON TV IS PRETTY INTERESTING.

MONOTO-NOUS WORK SUITABLE FOR ROBOTS? PLAYING FACTORY?!
I SEE, ALL THOSE ITEMS ARE AWAITING ASSEMBLY, RIGHT?

AH.
KNOCK
コ"

SIIGH
は〜あ
FORGET IT. I'M GONNA STUDY.
Not worth watching.

IT'S JUST SEKI MOVING STUFF AROUND.
BUT IN THE END,

I CAN'T GET IT BACK FROM THERE!
BUT SEKI HATES BEING INTERRUPTED DURING HIS GAMES...

MY ERAS-ER!
コロッ
BOUNCE
コトン
THMP

ミーン
HLLLSH
HE'S IGNOR-ING ME?! WHY?

MAYBE HE WON'T MIND?
OH, BUT HE'S USING THAT ROBOT ARM!

SAY, CAN YOU USE THAT TO PICK IT UP?
WHISPER
ヒソ
I DROPPED MY ERASER.
ヒソ
WHISPER
ヒソ
SEKI, SEKI!

DON'T TELL ME SEKI HAS
NO RE-SPONSE.

...
KTAK
カタン
KTAK
カタン

HMM, IS THAT SO.
I SEE, A MACHINE WOULDN'T HEAR VOICES.

HE'S FULLY TURNED INTO A PART OF AN INDUSTRIAL ROBOT!
TRANSFORMED ?!

CAN'T KILL THEIR EMOTIONS SO EASILY !!
THWAP
THWAP

AH, BUT HUMANS
RIP
RIP

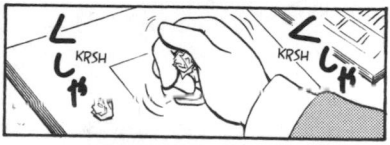
KRSH
KRSH

WHISPER
WHISPER
H-HEY, SEKI, YOU CAN HEAR ME, YES?
A- ARE YOU PISSED OFF?

WHACK
WHACK

KLNK
カクッ
KRIMP
クシャッ

TOSS
ポイッ
HE SIMPLY REMOVED THE FACTORY'S TRASH WITHOUT ANY HINT OF ANGER ?!
A COMPLETELY EMOTIONLESS ACTION...

DID SEKI TRULY
WIPE AWAY HIS SOUL ?!

HIS HUMAN SOUL, THAT IS!!
I SOME-HOW NEED TO GET SEKI TO RE-TRIEVE IT RIGHT AWAY.

WILL HE REVERT TO HIMSELF? BUT CLASS WILL BE OVER IF I JUST WAIT.
WHAT A BOTHER. I CAN'T TAKE NOTES WITHOUT MY ERASER...

OH, RIGHT!
SHK
カチャ
カチャ
SHK

BOUNCE
THUNK

I'M SOR-RY!
LOB

WHOMP
AH!
C'MON! REMEMBER LOVE, AND YOUR CARING HEART!
WELL? ISN'T IT CUTE? YOU LIKE CUTE THINGS, DON'T YOU, SEKI?
OH, IT'S STUCK!
DANGLE
NO, NO, DON'T THROW IT OUT!
AAAH, IT FAILED?!
SWFF
DANGLE
DANGLE
DANGLE
ARGH, DON'T BE SO ROUGH!
SWING
SWING

Are you back?!
AH, BUT THAT'S STILL A HUMAN QUALITY, NO?
I WAS CALLING BACK HIS KIND HEART BUT HIS CRUEL HEART CAME OUT INSTEAD!

AN EVIL FACE ?!
ニタア
SNEER

SEKI!

MY ERASER! GRAB IT!
!

?
?
サッ
SNATCH

?
THAT'S WHERE YOU SHOULD USE THE ROBOT ARM!
イラッ
IRK

59th Period

SEKI DOESN'T EVEN HAVE HIS BOOK OUT AGAIN.

THE ISLAND'S DWELLINGS, DUE TO POTABLE WATER,
ARE LOCATED IN BASINS IN THE RELATIVELY COLD NORTH COAST.

A GYM SUIT ?
WHY TAKE THEM OUT NOW...?

SLIP
ズルッ

HE PULLED OUT A PAIR OF JEANS. NOT SWEAT PANTS!
NO! THEY'RE JEANS!

SFF
す,

IS HE CHANGING INTO THEM AFTER SCHOOL TO STOP OFF SOME-WHERE?
?
BUT WHY?
?

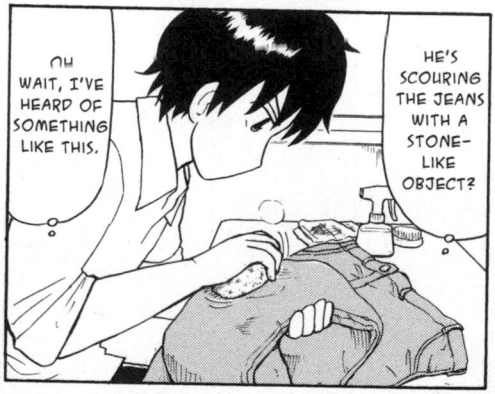
HE'S SCOURING THE JEANS WITH A STONE-LIKE OBJECT?
∩H WAIT, I'VE HEARD OF SOMETHING LIKE THIS.

!
SCRUB
SCRUB
ゴシゴシ

HE'S PUTTING THE FINAL TOUCH ON HIS OWN JEANS DURING CLASS?
WHAT REFINED FRIVOLOUSNESS!

"STONE-WASHING!"
THE METHOD DENIM CONNOISSEURS USE TO LIGHTEN THE SHADE TO MAKE THEM MORE FASHIONABLE?!

SEKI'S STREET CLOTHES ...
I DON'T RECALL HIM BEING FUSSY,
BUT NOW HE GETS FASHION?

BUT ISN'T STONE-WASHING JEANS PRETTY DIFFICULT?
IF YOU'RE INEXPERIENCED, THEY COULD COME OUT LOOKING DIRTY INSTEAD. IT TAKES CONFIDENCE.

HUH?
HUH?
NO WAY ...!!

CHAK
カチャッ

EEEEEEP!
ひゃあああ〜っ
HE CUT THEM?! HE'S PUTTING HOLES IN THEM?!
ZNIP
ちょキン

THAT'S TOO HEAVY A BLOW TO BEAR!
ONE MISTAKE AND YOU'LL RUIN THE PAIR!

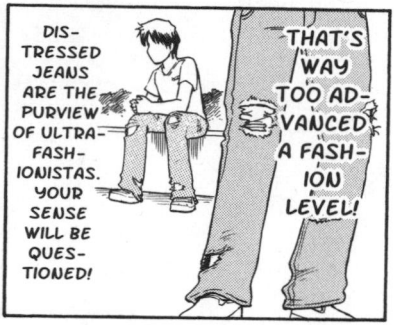
DIS-TRESSED JEANS ARE THE PURVIEW OF ULTRA-FASH-IONISTAS. YOUR SENSE WILL BE QUES-TIONED!
THAT'S WAY TOO AD-VANCED A FASH-ION LEVEL!

PEEK
チラッ

SHAKE
ブル
SHAKE
ブル
ZSH
ザシュッ
ZSH
ザシュッ
ZSH
ザシュッ

ZKISH
ザシュッ
WAAAAH!

WELL DONE !!

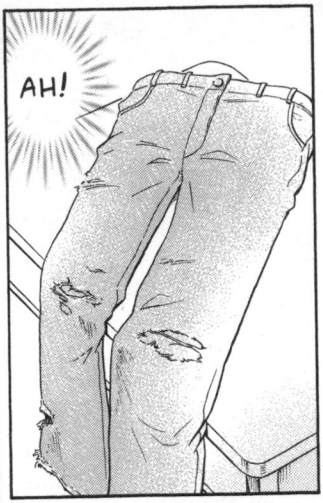
AH!

YOU'VE GOT QUITE THE FASHION SENSE, SEKI!
VERY STYLISH !
YOU'VE CHANGED MY MIND!

THEY HAVE A FEELING OF BEING WELL-WORN, PLUS THE HOLES OPENED AT THE KNEES ARE VERY NATURAL!
A HUE THAT'S NOT TOO HARSH, RETAINING QUALITY WHILE REMOVING STIFFNESS.

HM ?
ゴリ SHFF
ゴリ SHFF

I THINK IT LINES UP PERFECTLY, BUT...

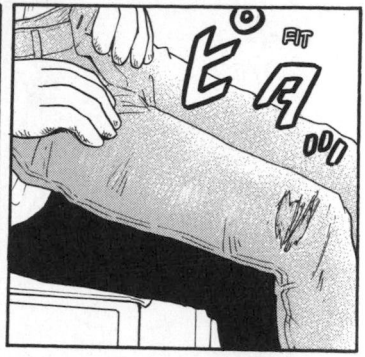
FIT
ピタ

はっ
GASP!

WHAT'S HE DOING UNDER THERE ...
SHFF
ゴソ
SHFF
ゴソ

...

NO... IS SEKI GONNA TRY THEM ON?!
A FIT-TING ?!
RUSTLE
ゴソゴソ
RUSTLE
ゴソ
RUSTLE
ゴソ

DON'T TAKE OFF YOUR PANTS NEXT TO ME, PLEASE!
AND TO BOOT, JEANS ARE BOTTOM WEAR!

BUT WE'RE AT SCHOOL, AND IN THE MIDDLE OF CLASS!!
I MEAN, IT'S TEMPTING TO PUT ON NEW CLOTHES ON RIGHT AWAY...

I AM SO NOT LOOKING!
TURN
STOP IT, SEKI, YOU IDIOT!

HUH? HE'S WEARING THEM?!

UH, IT GOT QUIET.
DID HE GIVE UP TRYING?

DON'T FREAK ME OUT LIKE THAT!
ふぅ～, WHEW
AW, GEEZ!

HE JUST ROLLED UP THE PANT LEGS AND SLIPPED THE JEANS ON?!
OH, HE DIDN'T TAKE HIS UNI-FORM PANTS OFF!

!!
OK, SEKI, PLEASE READ FROM PAGE 82.

GEEZ, YOU HAD MY HEART RACING.
WELL, I GUESS IT'S ENOUGH IF HE'S ONLY CHECK-ING THE KNEE HOLES.

...

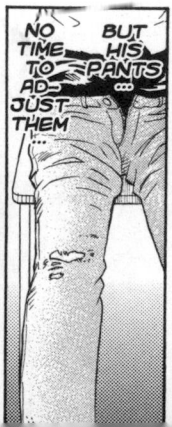
NO TIME TO AD-JUST THEM...
BUT HIS PANTS...

FLIP
OH, HE GOT IT OUT.
SEKI, YOUR TEXT-BOOK
SHWIP

HE STOOD UP LIKE THAT!!
WELL, IT'S TRUE THEY'RE NOT VISIBLE FROM THE FRONT.
カタッ
CLINK

IT'S A BIT OF A LET DOWN THAT YOU WISH YOU'D NEVER SEEN.
NO MATTER HOW FASHIONABLE A PERSON IS, IF YOU CATCH SIGHT OF THEIR SHABBY SIDE,
HEH HEH HEH

HOW IRONIC.
TO CUT SUCH A SAD FIGURE WHILE PURSUING STYLE...

カタッ
KLATTER
AH, YES!
スッ
SCF
YOKOI, READ THE NEXT PARAGRAPH.

YOU CAN STOP THERE.

ビリリッ
RRIP

HE SHOULDN'T HAVE PUT THOSE HOLES IN AFTER ALL...
OH, DEAR.
ずーん
GLOOM

THE TEAR GOT BIG-GER!!
Doesn't look so good...
GAPE
びろーん

JUST HOLD STILL!
HUH? WHAT?
プープ
GIGGLE
Where's that rip...

...
WHISPER
ヒソ
DONCHA THINK ...?
WAS THAT YOKOI JUST NOW?
ヒソ
WHISPER

60th Period
TODAY IS PARENT VISITING DAY.

IT'S NERVE-RACKING THINKING MY PARENTS ARE HERE.
チラッ
GLANCE

ガヤ
BLIB
ガヤ
HLIB

ALL RIGHT, QUIET DOWN!
I'LL BE CALLING ON A LOT OF YOU TODAY, SO PAY ATTENTION!
ガヤ
HLIB
ガヤ
BLIB

I WONDER IF I CAN ACTUALLY LEARN ANYTHING TODAY.
GEEZ, SO EMBARRASSING!

OH, STOP IT, MOM! DON'T WAVE AT ME!

WHEW!
AH, HE'S GOT HIS BOOKS OUT.

SO LONG AS SEKI DOESN'T DO ANYTHING WEIRD.

SHIFF
HM?

NO WAY YOU CAN GOOF OFF WITH SO MANY PEOPLE WATCHING.
EVEN MIGHTY SEKI...
THAT'S RIGHT.
HEH HEH HEH

SHE'S CLEARLY STANDING CLOSER THAN THE OTHER PARENTS!
WEIRD!
HUH? WHAT? SOMEONE'S STANDING RIGHT BEHIND ME.

ズオオオ
LOOOOM

IS IT SOMEONE I KNOW?
WHY ON EARTH?
チラッ
©JIZUKU

あっ
AH!

WHO IS SHE? HER FEATURES DO SEEM FAMILIAR ...
WHOA, WHAT A PRETTY LADY!

SHE'S SEKI'S MOTHER!
SHE MUST BE!

AND SHE'S MAD AT ME?
AT SEKI'S HOUSE.
BUT HERE I AM.
SHE FOUND OUT I TRES-PASSED ON HER HOUSE THE OTHER DAY...

DUH.
I SEE, SHE'S STANDING IN THAT ODD SPOT SO SHE CAN BE NEAR SEKI.

OH, COULD IT BE...
BUT WHY NEAR ME AND NOT NEXT TO SEKI?

...
クルン
TWIRL
クルン

SHE IS GLARING AT ME, RIGHT?
じっ
STARE
OOH, I FEEL A HARSH GAZE ON ME

AH!

IS PEN-SPIN-NING ?!
DON'T TELL ME TODAY'S GAME

THAT MUST BE WHAT HIS MOM IS WATCH-ING.
HE'S BEEN TWIRL-ING THAT PEN FOR A WHILE ...

BAD SEKI, SHOWING HER HOW IRRE-SPON-SIBLE YOU ARE! GEEZ!
POOR MOM, SHE MUST BE SO UNEASY.
BUT IT'S CLEARLY VISIBLE TO YOUR MOTHER!

IT'S SIMPLE, BUT LIKELY ONE OF THE FEW GAMES HE CAN DO TODAY.
FOR SURE, YOU CAN HIDE THAT SORT OF THING FROM PEOPLE BEHIND YOU, WITH YOUR BODY.

HM ?
FLITTER
ヒラッ

SHOULD I CHASTISE SEKI ON HIS MOTHER'S BEHALF AS WELL?
PER-HAPS ...
A grave responsibility!

COULD THAT BE...
THERE'S A RIBBON ATTACHED TO THE END OF HIS PEN...

THIS MOVE-MENT!
クルルン
TWIRL
AAH...
クルルン
TWIRL

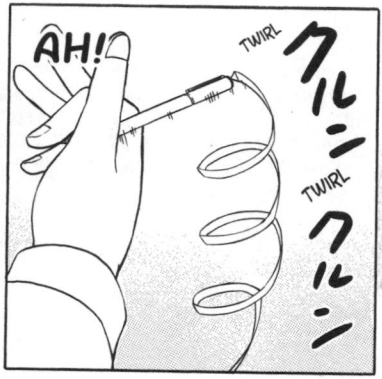
AH!
TWIRL
クルン
TWIRL
クルン

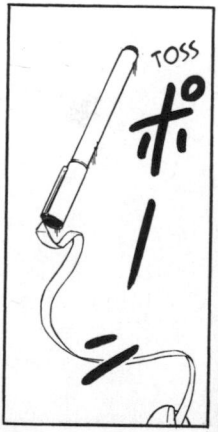
TOSS
ポーン

HE'S PER-FORM-ING A RIBBON ROUTINE WITH HIS PEN!!
RHYTHMIC GYMNAS-TICS!

WOW! HIS SKILL IS IMPRESSIVE, BUT THERE'S ARTISTRY, TOO!
WHO KNEW SUCH AN APPLICATION OF...
A FINISHING POSE!
SWAP

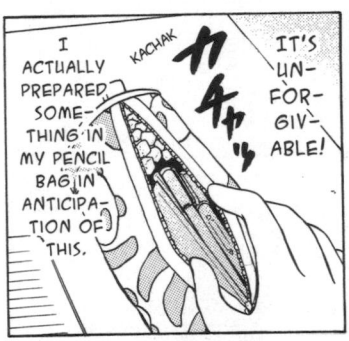
I ACTUALLY PREPARED SOMETHING IN MY PENCIL BAG IN ANTICIPATION OF THIS.
KACHAK
IT'S UNFORGIVABLE!

BUT YOU'RE STILL GOOFING AROUND AS MUCH AS YOU PLEASE, SEKI!
WAIT, NO!!

!
WASH
THWAP

I'LL INTERRUPT YOU WITH THESE!
BULLETS MADE OF ERASER BITS!

HUH ?!
GLARE
キッ
KLATTER
カタン
KLATTER
カタン

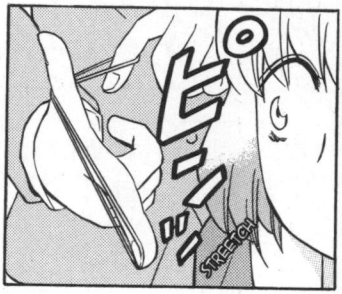
ビーン
STRETCH

HM ?!
B-BUT I HADN'T SHOT AT YOU YET!
わた わた
FLAIL
FLAIL
じ〜っ
STARE

ビ
SWPP
WHAAAT ?!!

OH, IS THAT WHY SHE'S STANDING NEXT TO ME?
FROM HERE SHE CAN WATCH HIS HANDS AND AIM AT HIM.

SEKI'S MOTHER SHOT HIM WITH A RUBBER BAND!
A RUB-BER BAND !!

KNOWS
MEANS HIS MOM

THE FACT THAT SHE BROUGHT RUBBER BANDS WITH HER
NO, WAIT A SEC.

SO THIS ISN'T THE FIRST OBSERVA-TION DAY WHERE HE'S PLAYED AROUND.
BLUSH
I CAN'T HELP IMAGIN-ING...

THAT SEKI'S ALWAYS GOOFING OFF IN CLASS!!

THE HISTORY OF HARDSHIP SUFFERED BY SEKI'S MOTHER!

HE'S GONNA KEEP AT IT? HE SHOWS NO REMORSE!
AH!
SNEAK
そそそっ

SEKI'S SO IMPOS-SIBLE!
GEEZ, IT'S NOT JUST ME; HE CAUSES HIS FAMILY TROUBLE, TOO.

KLATTER
カッシッ

THWAP
ビッ

AT HAN-DLING SEKI!
SHE'S A PRO

WHOA!
SHE STRUCK FIRST TO HINDER HIM.

A SPECIAL COM-MUNI-CATION STYLE JUST FOR SEKI!
TELLING HIM TO STUDY?
SHE'S TARGET-ING HIS TEXT-BOOK...
...
BUT HOW BOLD SHE IS AMONG SO MANY PEOPLE.
PING
PING

SFF

IT'S A BLIND ANGLE THAT HIS MOM CAN'T HIT!
OH, OVER THERE,

AH! HE'S PICKING UP HIS PEN?!
SHFF

ROLL
コロコロ
ROLL
ビシッ
THWAP
ピン
PING
HEH
フッ
...

LET YOU DO AS YOU PLEASE ANY-MORE !!
BAM
SEKI, WE WON'T

HE'S RIGHT BACK TO PEN-SPIN-NING!
ARGH ...
TWIRL
TWIRL

HEH
RUSTLE

I NEVER THOUGHT I'D SEE SUCH A SPLENDID DAY!
HIS FOOLING AROUND HAS BEEN FULLY SUP-PRESSED !
Ya! Ya!

THE RUBBER BAND WAS RE-PELLED ?!
No way!
PING

PLEASE, NAB HIM!
SNIP

HE MODIFIED THE PEN INTO A KENPO WEAPON!!
NUN-CHUCKS?!
WHIP
ARE THOSE...
IT'S NO ORDINARY PEN?!
KLINK
EVEN WITH THE TWO OF US WORKING TOGETHER WE CAN'T STOP SEKI...
UIRGH...
I CAN'T BELIEVE HE PREPARED SUCH A THING...
How skilled...
IF HE CAN DEFEND HIMSELF, WE CAN'T DO A THING!
WOOO
SPIN
SPIN

SHFF
すっ

SNAP
パ
SSS
ピシッ

♫
GRIKK
ぐっ

KASHAK
カシャン

AH!
THWAK
パシッ

WHOA !!

DON'T YOU DARE PICK IT UP!
PUIP
PUIP
SWAP
THWAP

IT TANGLED UP THE NUNCHUCKS AND MADE THEM FALL!
SHE CUT A RUBBER BAND AND TIED MY ERASER BITS TO THE ENDS TO MAKE A NEW WEAPON!

I'D LOVE TO LEARN HER DIVERSE ATTACKS !!
HOW BRIL-LIANT!

OH ?
ぷいっ
SNUB
...!

Yo-koi.
HEH HEH
WERE THE TWO OF US TOO MEAN TO HIM?
HE'S SULK-ING?

SOLVE THIS PROB-LEM.
...HUH?
IT'S EASY, RIGHT?

YOU'RE SMILING, SO YOU MUST KNOW.
YOKOI!

Hunh?!
TREMBLE
ブル
TREMBLE
ブル
!-!...
WASN'T PAYING ATTEN-TION.

ガタタッ
KLATTER

RECESS.

OH, MOM!
...
GIGGLE
クス
GIGGLE
クス
GIGGLE
クス
WAAAH!

I'M SO SORRY TO HAVE EMBAR-RASSED YOU!

SHIFF
BLIB
WELL, I'LL BE GOING.
OK.
HUIB
JUST PAY ATTEN-TION TO CLASS THIS AFTER-NOON.
IT'S OKAY, I'M NOT MAD.
M-MRS. SEKI ...?
AH!
SHE'S SUR-PRIS-INGLY SHY.
WHAT IS THIS ?
HUH? WAIT!
DASH
HUH?
HUH?
THRUST

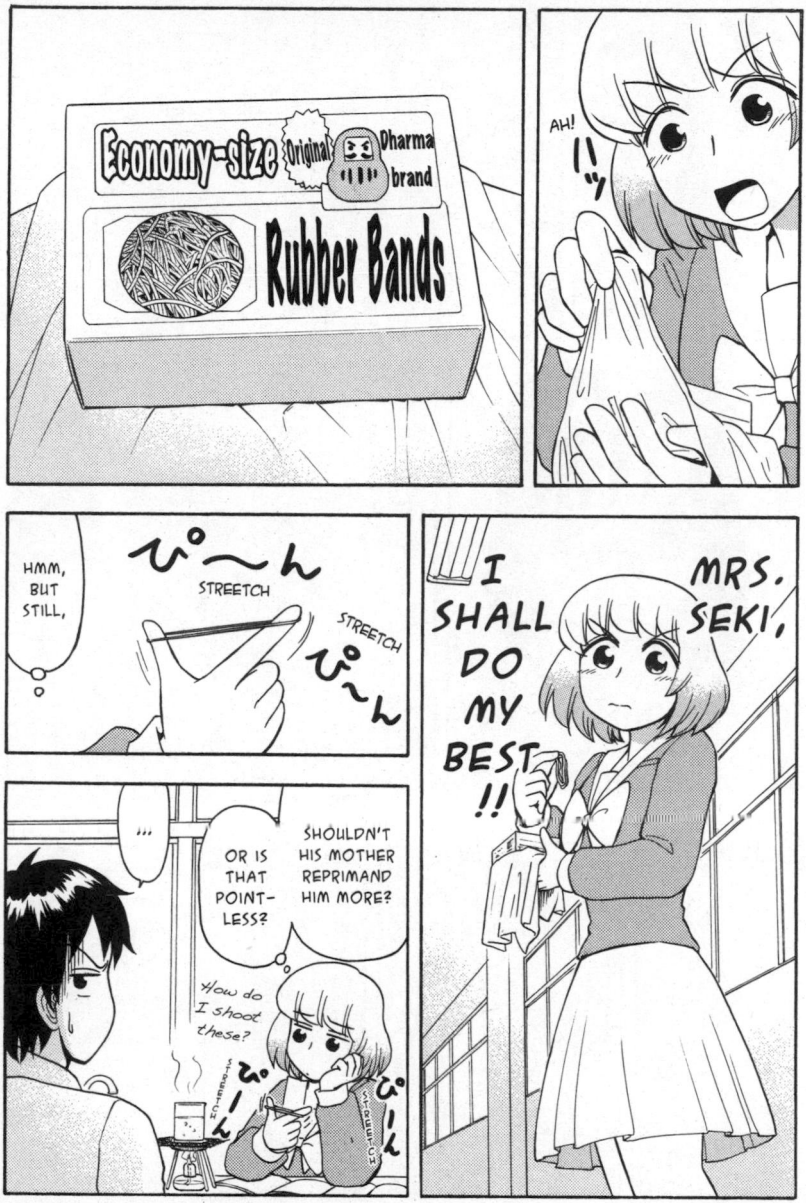
Economy-size
Original
Dharma brand
Rubber Bands
AH!
HMM, BUT STILL,
ぴ～ん
STREETCH
STREETCH
ぴ～ん
I SHALL DO MY BEST!!
MRS. SEKI,
...
OR IS THAT POINT-LESS?
SHOULDN'T HIS MOTHER REPRIMAND HIM MORE?
How do I shoot these?
ぴーん
ぴーん

My Neighbor Seki

• 61st Period •
MORN-ING!
YO!
WOW!

AMAZ-ING!
SUCH GREAT FLOWERS IN YOUR GARDEN?
I GREW THEM IN OUR GARDEN WITH MY MOTHER'S HELP.

WHAT PRETTY FLOWERS! DID YOU BRING THEM, GOTO?
AH, YES!

HOW LOVELY... I WISH I COULD GARDEN, TOO.
I WANT TO TRY IT SOMEDAY...

サアアア
SHAAAA

HE BEAT ME TO IT.

HOW CAN YOU GARDEN ON YOUR DESK DURING CLASS?!
I REFUSE TO BE IMPRESSED, EVEN THOUGH YOU'RE A BOY. OR RATHER...

NOT REALLY SOMETHING WORTH QUARRELING OVER.
WELL, FLOWERS IN THE CLASS-ROOM ISN'T ALL THAT BAD.

TEE HEE

HEY NOW! I DON'T THINK THAT'S A FREE-USE SPACE?
THOUGH IT IS PICTUR-ESQUE.

KTAK
AH, HE'S PUT SOME ON THE WINDOW-SILL, TOO!

ARE ACTUALLY REPUR-POSED PLASTIC BOTTLES?!
UPON CLOSER INSPEC-TION, THOSE TINY, PRETTY PLANT POTS

はっ GASP!

I NEED TO GET ANGRY AND START PRESSUR-ING HIM NOW.
THAT'S RIGHT. KNOWING SEKI, HE MIGHT ESCALATE IT FURTHER.

SEKI'S GARDENING IN AN EARTH-FRIENDLY MANNER!
HOW ECO-FRIENDLY!!

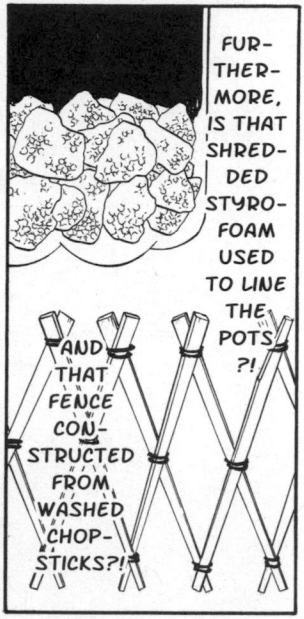
FURTHERMORE, IS THAT SHREDDED STYROFOAM USED TO LINE THE POTS?!
AND THAT FENCE CONSTRUCTED FROM WASHED CHOPSTICKS?!

FSH
す、

AH!
HOIST
そお、

BEING ECO-CONSCIOUS, HE'S LIKE A CLEVER HAUSFRAU ...
IT'S COMMENDABLE, SO I'M HESITANT TO REPRIMAND HIM LIKE USUAL. PLUS IT'S GREEN.

A CLEARLY ANNOYING ACT!
HE'S EXPANDING THE GARDEN WITH A RACK OFF THE BACK OF MAEDA'S CHAIR!

STOP IT, SEKI!
YOU'RE BOTHERING MAEDA!
ECO-FRIENDLY OR NOT, I GOTTA STOP HIM!

THAT HE'D BOTHER PEOPLE WHO ARE STUDYING HARD!
THIS IS EXACTLY WHAT I WAS AFRAID OF—

HRM ?
にへらっ
BEAM

...

SHFF
ささっ

TO HIS GARDEN EXPANSION... I DUNNO ...
BUT BY ACCEPTING, I'M GIVING TACIT CONSENT

HUH? WHAT?
HE'S WILLING TO GIFT ME THIS PLANT?
ARE YOU SURE?

FLOWERS ON MY DESK PUTS ME AT EASE...
HAVING LOTS OF FLOWERS AROUND SURE IS THE BEST.

SKRITCH
カリ
SKRITCH
カリ
SKRITCH
カリ

ぴょっ
TAP

ぴ～ん
SPRING

FLAIL
バタバタ
FLAIL
バタッ
FLAIL

ゼェ
WHEEZE
ゼェ
WHEEZE

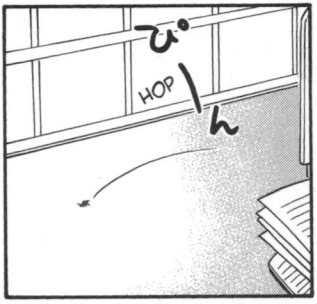
ぴょん
HOP

GEEZ, IT'S SO UNLIKE SEKI...
HM ?
WAIT A MINUTE, I THINK I'VE HEARD OF THIS.

SEKI! BUGS! BUGS!
YOU CAN'T BRING SUCH THINGS INTO CLASS!

INSECTS ARE UN-AVOIDABLE IF ONE IS BEING KIND TO NATURE AND NOT USING PESTICIDES ...
ORGANIC !!

KACHAK
ジャラッ

I GOTTA PUT UP WITH THE BUGS, AT LEAST...
'CAUSE IT'S ECO-FRIEND-LY.
SO ECO-CON-SCIOUS...
SHAKE
プル
SHAKE
プル

...
ちま
FIDDLE
ちま
FIDDLE

SNAP
キッ
KRIK
メキ
KRIK
メキ

THOSE WERE BRAND-NEW CHOP-STICKS?
I TOTALLY THOUGHT YOU WERE REPUR-POSING USED ONES...!

SHOVE
I DON'T WANT THIS ANY MORE!

YOU'RE BEING ANTI-GREEN!
WHAT A WASTE OF WOOD RE-SOURC-ES!

!
STRETCH

PUT ALL OF THAT AWAY, STAT!
Bugs
Bugs
YOU'RE NOT THINKING ABOUT OTHERS AT ALL!

AIEEE!
THWAK

CLEAN IT UP OR I'LL USE THIS...
GRIK
GRIK
A RUBBER BAND I GOT FROM YOUR MOM!

OH, NO...
PING

...
WHAT SHOULD I DO? APOLOGIZE?
He's gonna yell at me...

I ACCIDENTALLY HIT MAEDA.
さっ
IS IT OBVIOUS FROM THE ANGLE THAT IT WAS ME?!

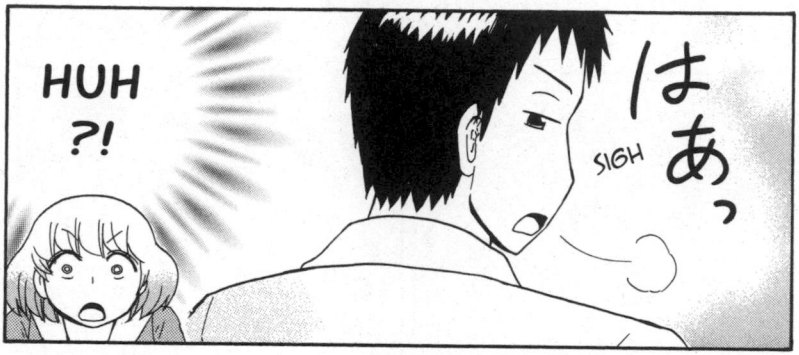
HUH ?!
はあっ
SIGH

I WONDER WHAT MAEDA THINKS OF ME...
OOOH...
うう
HUH?!
NO WAY! A LOVE TRIANGLE?!

HE JUST SIGHS, WITHOUT ANY SURPRISE OR SUSPICION?!
IS HE JUST TOTALLY RESIGNED ?!
WHY DID HE HAVE THAT REACTION ?

NOW THEN, NEXT ...

MAKE SURE YOU REMEMBER THAT.
THE CONSTITUTION AND INSTITUTIONS WERE CRITICAL IN THIS ERA.
• 62nd Period •

IS THAT, UM, AN INKWASH PAINTING?

STARE
じ〜〜〜

OH, HE'S PUTTING IT AWAY.
ROLL
クル
ROLL
クル

IS TODAY'S GAME ART APPRECIATION?
HE'S LOOKING AT IT VERY INTENTLY.
THAT'D BE NICE AND QUIET.

WHAAAAAT?!
ピラ
¥8,000-
FLIP
SKRIT
サラ
サラ
SKRIT

IS THAT WHY HE WAS STARING SO HARD AT IT? SO IS THIS GAME NOT APPRECIATION, BUT...
HE PUT A PRICE ON THE PAINT-ING?!

HE'S JUST IMITATING AN APPRAISER LIKE THE ONES ON TV, RIGHT?
THERE'S NO WAY HE CAN REALLY DO THAT.

ART APPRAISAL ?!

*Note: 1 yen is about 1 U.S. cent.

GACHNK
ガチャン
ZWSH
ザァァ
AAAH!

700 YEN?! IT'S THAT CHEAP?
NO WAY, IT'S GOTTA BE WORTH MORE!

HE TREATS THEM CARELESSLY ONCE HE'S SET THE PRICES...
IT'S STILL A NICE TEACUP, EVEN IF IT'S CHEAP.

WELL, THAT LOOKS LIKE NOTHING MORE THAN A WEIRD GLASS BOWL.
I CAN'T SEE HOW IT COULD BE WORTH MUCH.
STARE
STARE
What poor taste

...
プル
SHAKE
プル
SHAKE

チィン
KACHING
¥3,000,000-
3 MIL-LION YEN ?!

はー
HAA

HM ?!
000000
サラ
SKRIT
サラ
SKRIT

A LIE, IT'S GOTTA BE A LIE!!
NO, NO, THERE'S NO WAY YOU HAVE SOMETHING SO EXPEN-SIVE!!

HM ?

I'M FOCUS-ING ON CLASS.
HOW IDIOTIC. I CAN'T KEEP UP.

IT DOES LOOK SIMILAR ...
SHO-SOIN TREA-SURES?
GLASS VESSELS THAT TRAV-ELED THE SILK ROAD.

KNOWING SEKI, HE COULD'VE RESEARCHED THE INFO BEFORE-HAND.
WHICH MEANS THAT BOWL...

SUCH OBJECTS WOULD OBVIOUSLY BE WORTH A LOT.
I MEAN, THEY'RE IMPORTANT ENOUGH TO APPEAR IN A HISTORY TEXTBOOK.

THOUGH SEKI'S FAMILY MIGHT'VE EXCAVATED OLD THINGS FROM SOME-WHERE.
I CAN'T COMPLETELY DISMISS THE POSSIBILITY...

DON'T TELL ME... IT'S GENU-INE?
BUT HOW'D HE ACQUIRE A 3 MILLION YEN BOWL ...?

WHAT KIND OF TREA-SURE IS IT?!
OH? THERE'S ONE MORE ITEM!
TINK
コト

THAT MUST BE HAND-MADE.
OH, HOW CUTE!

GOOD LUCK WITH WORK!
MAKO

AH!

HM? HE LOOKS PAINED.
...

IT BRINGS TO MIND IMAGES OF A WARM HOUSE-HOLD.
I BET A LITTLE GIRL GAVE IT TO HER BELOVED FATHER.

THERE MUST'VE BEEN SOME PAINFUL CIRCUM-STANCE FOR THEM TO PART WITH A SENTI-MENTAL ITEM...
I WONDER IF THEY FOUND IT AT A BAZAAR OR SOME-THING.

NORMALLY PEOPLE WOULDN'T SELL SUCH A PRECIOUS THING.
BUT HOW DID SOMETHING LIKE THAT END UP WITH A STRANGER?
GOOD LUCK WITH WORK! MAKO

MY MIND'S VEERING OFF IN A BAD DIRECTION!
STOP, STOP!
ARGH, NO, NO!
House For Sale

キュポッ
SPOP

SEKI MUST BE STRUG-GLING TO APPRAISE IT.
YOU CAN'T REALLY PUT A PRICE ON SUCH ITEMS.

TOSS
ROLL
ROLL
ポイッ
ゴロ
ゴロ
SEKI, YOU MONEY GRUBBER!
YOU DON'T CARE IF IT WON'T MAKE YOU MONEY?!
HE WROTE THE PRICE DIRECTLY ON IT!!
GOOD LUCK WITH YOUR WORK! MAKO
BOOM
And just 1 yen?!
SKFF
スチャッ
RUSTLE
RUSTLE
ゴソ
ゴソ
HE LOOKED GLUM 'CAUSE IT HAS NO CASH VALUE.
SCRUB
SCRUB
ゴシ
ゴシ
ONE YEN, RIGHT?
IN THAT CASE, I'LL TAKE IT OFF YOUR HANDS.

WHA-AA?!
GOOD LUCK WITH WORK! AKO
¥700-
パロン
TA-DAA

I WANT THAT OTHER CUP AT THE SAME PRICE!
I DON'T WANT IT IF IT'S 700 YEN!
!

ぶん ぶん
SHAKE SHAKE
MARKING IT UP IS UNFAIR! WHAT A RIP-OFF!
IT WAS 1 YEN JUST A MINUTE AGO!!

IT'S TOTALLY ARBITRARY AFTER ALL!!
NONE OF THE PRICES WERE SET IN STONE!
...

HEY!!
SHFF
¥8,000-

63rd Period
AH!
KTNK
カタン
RUSTLE
ゴソ
RUSTLE
ゴソ
THIS MAY BE THE FIRST ONE I'VE SEEN.
HM? BUT I FEEL LIKE MY BROTHER DIDN'T HAVE ANY.
THAT'S SUCH A TYPICAL TOY FOR BOYS.
IS TODAY'S GAME MODEL TRAINS ...?
A TRAIN ...

WHOA!
KATAK
カタン

GACHA
ガチャ
GACHA
ガチャ

IT'LL DEFINITELY BE VERY IMPRESSIVE ...
GIVEN HIS ABILITIES, IF SEKI BUILDS A MODEL RAILWAY,

HE'S REALLY GONNA MOVE THEM...
HE EVEN HAS RAIL TRACKS.

I GOTTA STUDY WHILE I WAIT.
NO, NO, I CAN'T JUST SIT AND STARE AT HIM!

は、
GASP

じ〜っ
STARE
KOHAK
カチャ
KOHAK
カチャ

GLANCE
チラッ
SHOULD BE DONE BY NOW...

TIK
TOK

カリ
SKRITCH
カリ
SKRITCH

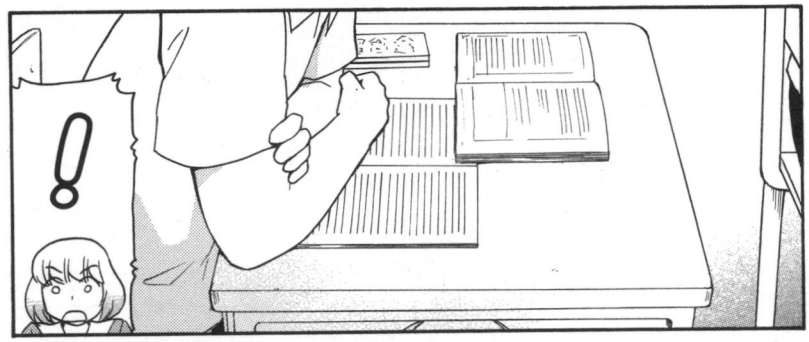
!

WHERE'S THE TRAIN?
HE PUT IT AWAY? HIS TEXTBOOK AND NOTEBOOK ARE OUT... WHAT GIVES?

HUH ...?

KTAN
ガタン
KTUN
ゴトン

THIS IS NO TIME TO BE MEEK!
THE TEACHER'S NOT HERE YET. IT'S STILL SAFE!
IT'S FINE, IT'S FINE!

?!
KTAN
ガタン
KTUN
ゴトン
KTAN
ガタン
KTUN
ゴトン

AM I HEARING THINGS? SOUNDS LIKE MOVEMENT COMING FROM SEKI'S...

HE'S RUNNING THAT MODEL TRAIN INSIDE HIS DESK?! DON'T TELL ME IT'S...
KTAN
ガタン
KTUN
ゴトン
KTUN
ゴトン
KTAN
ガタン
DESK!

HE REPRODUCED A SUBWAY INSIDE HIS DESK?!
A SUB-WAY ?!

HE LOOKS LIKE HE'S HAVING FUN?
AH !

HOW COULD THAT BE ANY FUN?!
BUT YOU CAN'T SEE THE TRAINS RUNNING AT ALL!
KTUN
KTAN

SIGH
I SEE... SEKI MUST REALLY BE A TRAIN GEEK, IF THAT'S ENOUGH FOR HIM.

KTAN
KTUN
LETS HIM PICTURE THE INVISIBLE TRAIN ...?
THE MUTED SOUNDS AND VIBRA-TIONS FROM THE DESK

YOU'RE TOO SELFISH, SEKI! YOU NEVER THINK ABOUT THOSE AROUND YOU!
IT'S SO WRONG TO SHOW ME ALL THOSE PARTS, YET NOT DISPLAY THEM IN ACTION!

IF I CAN'T WATCH IT GO ROUND AND ROUND!
BUT IT'S NOT FUN FOR ME

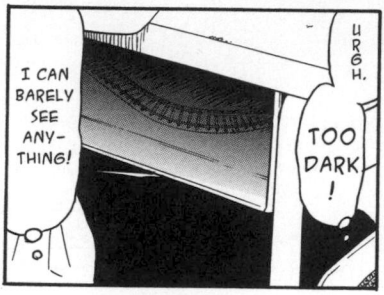
I CAN BARELY SEE ANY-THING!
URGH.
TOO DARK!

WOW! IT'S GOT ...ITS... LIGHTS ON...
ガタン KTAN
OH, IS THAT IT?!
ゴトン KTUN

KREAK ギシッ
KREAK ギッシ

BULLY! ARE YOU DELIBERATELY BLOCKING MY VIEW SO I CAN'T SEE?!
WHY'D YOU COVER IT?! MEANIE!

AAAH!!
SHIFF
すっ

IS IT SOME TRAIN PART?
HM? HE'S LOOKING INTENTLY AT SOME-THING...

じーっ
STARE

A HOLE!!
HE'S PEERING INTO AN AIR VENT HE MADE?

!
KTAN KTUN
KTAN KTUN

SO HE'S HAPPILY WATCHING HIS CREATION AFTER ALL!!
HE'S WATCHING THE SUBWAY RUSH BY!!

I'M DISAPPOINTED IN SEKI...
SLUMP
I'M NOT TALKING TO HIM ANY MORE.
♪ ♫

I STILL CAN'T SEE IT!
BUT WHY LOOK THROUGH A HOLE?

えっ
HUH?
ALL OF YOU SITTING IN THE VERY BACK ROW, COME ON UP.

TO WRAP UP, LET'S HAVE YOU SOLVE PARTS 1 TO 5
OF THE FIRST PROBLEM AT THE BLACKBOARD.

ガタッ
FOR THAT TO HAP-PEN...
KLATTER

I CAN WATCH THE TRAIN ALL I WANT!
I CAN LOOK INSIDE SEKI'S DESK IF HE'S GONE!

TRAIN!
TAK
TAK
TAK
TRAIN!

FASTER THAN SEKI!
I GOTTA SOLVE THE PROBLEM QUICKLY!

!
WHY DON'T YOU TACKLE THE 2ND PROBLEM AS WELL?

THAT WAS TOO EASY FOR YOU, EH, YOKOI.
YES!
CORRECT. WELL DONE.

OH, UH, IT'S OKAY IF YOU CAN'T SOLVE IT.
URGH!

GLARE
キロッ
FLINCH
ビクッ

OH, RIGHT ON TIME!
キーンコーンカーンコーン
DING DONG DING DONG
WAAAA AAAH!!
KOHAK
カチャ
KOHAK
カチャ
RUSTLE
ゴソ
RUSTLE
ゴソ

SIGH
はー
AH, CORRECT!
EXCELLENT, YOKOI, YOU DID WELL.

AFTER SCHOOL
HUH? YOKOI LEFT ALREADY?
SHE SAID SHE'S GOING TO WATCH TRAINS AT THE STATION.
She rushed off.
SHE'S INTO THAT?!

I HATE YOU ALL!!

64th Period

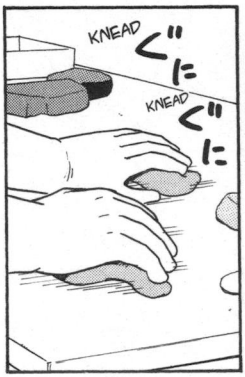
KNEAD ぐに
KNEAD ぐに

SKRITCH カリ
SKRITCH カリ

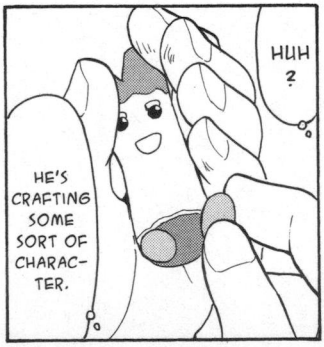
HUH ?
HE'S CRAFTING SOME SORT OF CHARAC-TER.

CLAY ?
ANOTHER GRADE SCHOOL TOY...
Colored...

トン…
TMP
UH, ISN'T THAT...

WHICH ONE?
I BET SEKI CAN 100% ACCURATELY RECREATE ANY OF THEM.

AH, HE'S DONE?
ふぅっ
WHEW

IT LOOKS LIKE A LEEK. IS IT AN ORIGINAL?
SORRY, BUT THAT'S NOT VERY INTERESTING.

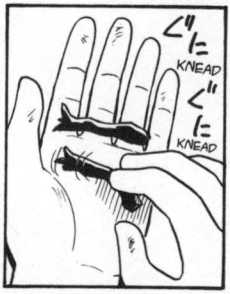
ぐに
KNEAD
ぐに
KNEAD

ぷちっ
SNAP

I DUNNO!
I HAVE NO IDEA WHO THAT IS.

...

THERE'S MORE!
AH!

OOH!
ギッ
GLARE
ジッ

AND THE OTHER ...
STILL NONE THAT I KNOW.

IS IT A TREE? SOME SORT OF PINE? IT HAS A CUTENESS FACTOR OF ZERO.
WHAT'S WITH THAT SIN-ISTER MON-STER? SCARY!

ZUMMM
ズ
オ
ー
オ
オ

LEEK ...
AND PINE?
HM?

SEKI'S CREATING NEW CHARACTERS FOR OUR TOWN!
I SEE! THESE ARE LOCAL MASCOTS, A CURRENT TREND!

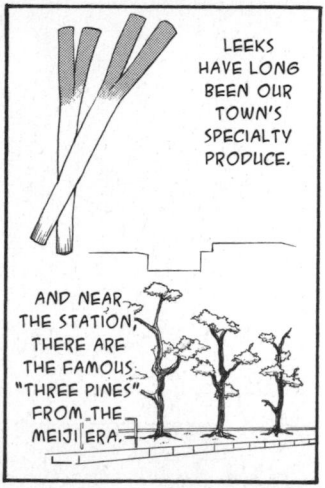
LEEKS HAVE LONG BEEN OUR TOWN'S SPECIALTY PRODUCE.
AND NEAR THE STATION, THERE ARE THE FAMOUS "THREE PINES" FROM THE MEIJI ERA.

I DIDN'T KNOW HE HAD SUCH LOVE FOR HIS HOMETOWN.
I SEE. WELL DONE, WELL DONE!
HEH
HEH
HEH

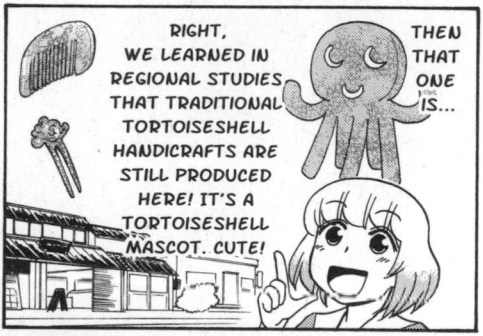
RIGHT, WE LEARNED IN REGIONAL STUDIES THAT TRADITIONAL TORTOISESHELL HANDICRAFTS ARE STILL PRODUCED HERE! IT'S A TORTOISESHELL MASCOT. CUTE!
THEN THAT ONE IS...

HE'S FANNING THE MASCOTS?
パタ FLAP
パタ FLAP

ピッ
FWP
Cool

KLUNK
パ
ク
ッ
ポ
ン
ポ

AH !
グラッ
TEETER

LEAVE IT TO SEKI TO THINK AHEAD ...
HE REALLY WANTS TO TURN THEM INTO COSTUMES !

THEY NEED TO BE DESIGNED TO WITHSTAND STRONG WINDS FOR SAFETY.
OH RIGHT, PEOPLE IN MASCOT COSTUMES OFTEN DO PROMO-TION WORK OUT-DOORS.

"REJECTS?!" THEY'RE NOT ALL GONNA BE MASCOTS TOGETHER ?!
HE'S NAR-ROWING THEM DOWN?
Rejects

TOSS
ポイ
HUNH ?!
Rejects
Rejects

A FIGHT TO THE DEATH WHERE ONLY ONE WILL SURVIVE?!
A LOCAL MASCOT BATTLE?!

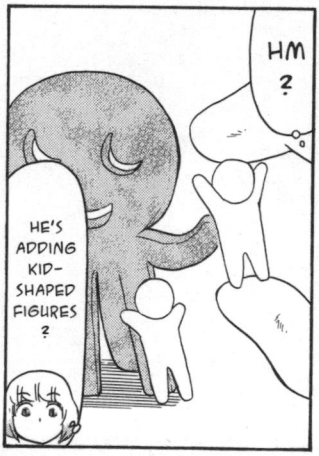
HM?
HE'S ADDING KID-SHAPED FIGURES?

NO ONE WILL MIND MULTIPLE MASCOTS.
YOU DON'T HAVE TO MAKE IT SO CUTTHROAT.

I TOTALLY ENDORSE TORTIE AND AM AGAINST THREE PINES!!
BUT WITH THE LEEK REJECTED, THERE ARE TWO LEFT.

WOW!
ちょこーん
CHILL

THAT'S A KEY REQUIREMENT TO BE A LOVABLE MASCOT.
I SEE, HE'S TESTING IF IT CAN HANDLE LOTS OF KIDS.

ひょいっ
HOIST

I CAN TOTALLY SEE TORTIE BEING LOVED BY CHILDREN!
キャッ
YAY
YAY
キャッ
PLAY-ING WITH KIDS SUITS IT WELL!

HM ?
WAIT, WHY?! IT HASN'T LOST YET...

WHAAT?!
ポイッ
TOSS
Rejects
Rejec

フォッ
HO
フォ
HO
フォ
HO
S-SURE, IT'S CAR-RYING MORE KIDS...
BUT IT JUST LOOKS LIKE A PHAN-TOM KIDNAP-PER TO ME!

EEE EEP !!
GLOMPP
カバッ

シャキーン
TA-DAA
Official Selection
Official Selection
PEEL
ピラッ
HM ?
OUR TOWN MAS-COT...
THAT EVIL THREE PINES IS OUR TOWN MASCOT ?!
NO WAY!! I REFUSE TO AC-KNOW-LEDGE IT!!
あ
あ
あ
あ
WAAAAH
I KNOW !
SKRITCH
カリ
カリ
カリ
SKRITCH
ばっ
SHOVE
♫

むっ HRM.
MATH TEST
Rumi Yokoi

WELL? PINE MASCOTS THAT I CAME UP WITH.
THEY'RE THE "FRIENDLY PINE BROTHERS."

KNEAD
ムに
SNAP
ぷちっ
KNEAD
ムに

IF YOU'RE GONNA HAVE A COMPETITION, LET MINE PARTICIPATE, TOO!
ALL RESIDENTS HAVE THE RIGHT TO SUBMIT MASCOT IDEAS!

はーあ
SIIGH

WE ABSO-LUTELY CAN'T LOSE!
NOW, LET'S DECIDE OUR TOWN'S TRUE MASCOT !!

HEY, YOU DON'T NEED TO CHANGE THEM!
what is that?
WHISPER
ヒソ
SEKI, YOU GOT THEM WRONG.
ヒソ
WHISPER
?!

HUH ?
ぐてえっ
WILT

JUST COPY THIS, OKAY?
ヒソ
WHISPER
WHISPER
ヒソ
MAKE THEM EXACTLY LIKE MY DRAWING!
That's weird
...

SPLACH
どぢゃっ

My Neighbor Seki

TODAY, WE ARE DISCUSSING OUR FREE TIME SCHEDULES BY GROUP.
IT'S ALMOST FIELD TRIP TIME.
Field Trip Guidebook

ガヤ
BLIB
ガヤ
HLIB
65th Period

COULD YOU PLEASE JOIN THE DISCUSSION?
C'MON BOYS, ARE YOU LISTENING?
Nod

HM?
FLUTTER
ピラッ

OOH, I DEFINITELY WANNA GO HERE.
FORGET IT, LET'S JUST CHOOSE ON OUR OWN.
ワイ
CHATTER
ワイ
CHATTER

Trip Guidebook
Trip Guidebook
Trip Guidebook
?!

LITTLE THINGS FELL OUT OF SEKI'S GUIDE ...
?

COMING ALONG ON OUR TRIP?!
THE ROBOT FAMILY IS
Trip Guidebook

GASP
はっ

SKFF

ARE THOSE TOY-SIZED GUIDES? WHICH MEANS...

LOTS OF NICE SHOPS AROUND HERE.
WHERE DO YOU WANNA GO?
HERE, I BROUGHT OVER THE GUIDE-BOOK.
HUH? SORRY. WHAT'S UP?

HEY, YOU LISTEN-ING?
RUMI.

ZOO
A ZOO CLOSE BY, TOO?
HM? THERE'S ...
SCHOOL

HMM, LET'S SEE...

THIS LOOKS FUN!
THIS!

A ZOO !!

YOU CAN GO TO A ZOO ANY-WHERE.
えーと
LET'S GO TO A TRENDIER PLACE!
えーと
RURUMU Shinchu
NO WAY!
SO UNCOOL.
HUH?!
HM? THERE'S AN APPLE ORCHARD NEARBY?
APPLE ORCHARD When in season, you can pick your own!
AND YOU CAN PICK THEM ...
APPLE PICK-ING!
COULD BE FUN...
OH NO, I DON'T THINK SO.
YOU SOUND LIKE A MOTHER.
It's not a family trip!
MAMA YOKOI?
WHAAAAT?!!
IT'S ALL YOUR FAULT!
?
AND SO, THE DAYS WENT BY

UNTIL FINALLY, IT WAS THE FIRST DAY OF THEIR TRIP.

ガヤ YAMMER
...
ガヤ YAMMER

WHISPER ヒソ ヒソ
YOU OUGHT TO SIT NEXT TO SEKI...
I STILL REALLY FEEL BAD, YOKOI!

OH, WANT A GUMMY?
WE'RE IN DIFFERENT GROUPS, BUT AT LEAST WE GET TO RIDE TOGETHER, GOTO!

IF I SIT BETWEEN THEM NO ONE WILL SUSPECT ANYTHING.
O-OH, RIGHT, THEIR RELA-TIONSHIP IS STILL A SECRET...

IN FACT, I'D RATHER HAVE SOMEONE BETWEEN US.
WHY? IT'S FINE.

?
GOT IT! I'LL HARDEN MY HEART AND BE A DIVIDING WALL BETWEEN YOU TWO!

AND WITH SO MANY EYES ON THE BUS, THEY'D RISK BEING FOUND OUT!
IF THE LOVING COUPLE SAT SIDE BY SIDE, THEY'D END UP ALL LOVEY-DOVEY!

ゴオ
オオ
VROOOM

CHATTER
ワイ
ワイ
CHATTER
ワイ

MORE AND MORE NODDED OFF, PERHAPS SLEEP DEPRIVED FROM ANTICIPATION...
IT QUIETED DOWN AFTER 2 HOURS, AS IF THEY HAD WORN THEMSELVES OUT.

AH, GOTO'S FALLEN ASLEEP, TOO.
ZZZ すー
ZZZ すー

OH, BUT MAYBE IT'S...
THE ROBOT FAMILY ?!

SEKI'S PLAYING AROUND ?!
CAN'T YOU SIMPLY ENJOY A SCHOOL TRIP?

WHAAA?!
ゴソ RUSTLE
ゴソ RUSTLE

HE'S MAKING A GOOD-WEATHER CHARM ?
SO IT WON'T RAIN DURING OUR TRIP ?

AH !
TMBL

どさっ
ZHFF
HUH? HE'S MADE QUITE A FEW...
HE STAYED UP TO MAKE THEM THIS WHOLE TIME?
HE MUST REALLY BE LOOKING FORWARD TO THE TRIP.

I APPRECIATE THAT, BUT...
HA HA
A slight let-down
TO STILL BELIEVE IN SUCH A CHARM IS CHILDISH, YET THAT SUITS HIM...

ぎゅうっ
SQUEEZE
HM?

HE DID MAKE PLENTY OF THEM.
OH, HE'S PUTTING THEM AWAY.
ギュッ
PINCH

ガサッ
RUSTLE

IT DOES SEEM LIKE IT'D BE MORE EFFECTIVE THAN A REGULAR CHARM...
HE WAS MAKING SO MANY OF THE SMALL ONES TO USE AS STUFFING?

HE MADE AN EXTRA-LARGE CHARM?!
HE GATHERED THEM ALL TOGETHER!

AH!
...

PAUSE
ピタッ

OF COURSE YOU GOT CAR SICK, GEEZ...
IT'S 'CAUSE YOU'RE DOING DETAILED WORK IN A MOVING BUS.
TREMBLE
ブル
TREMBLE
ブル

SEKI GOT CAR SICK?!
HE'S ILL?!
プル
TREMBLE
プル
TREMBLE

...

!
ズルッ
SLIP

WHOA!
ゴソゴソ
RUMMAGE

HE MESSED UP ITS FACE?
YOU'RE PUSHING IT, ON A MOVING BUS WHILE STILL ILL.
ふら
SWAY
ふら
SWAY
SNIP
プツン
WHMP
わさっ

THAT'S TOTALLY UNNECESSARY FOR A FIELD TRIP!
せっ
TUG
せっ
TUG
せっ
TUG
HE HAS THAT MUCH EXTRA MATERIAL ?!

THEN AGAIN, SEKI READILY BELIEVES IN THE OCCULT, SO MAYBE THAT'S NOT TOO FAR OFF THE MARK.
HE'S LIKE AN ARTIST CARVING A STATUE OF BUDDHA WITH ALL HIS SOUL.

ピル
RUMBLE
ピル
RUMBLE

IT'S JUST A WEATHER DOLL'S FACE.
HE'S BEING SO FUSSY.
ブン
SHAKE
ブン
SHAKE
バサッ
FWAP

IS HE DONE ...?
HUH ?

SEKI'S RUN OUT OF STEAM ?!
OH !
ぐてっ
SLUMP

I CAN SENSE THE SOUL THAT SEKI PUT INTO IT!
Good job!
I'VE NEVER SEEN SUCH A DIGNIFIED WEATHER DOLL BEFORE!

HOW
D-DIVINE!!

ゴトン
GTUNK
ガタン
GTANK

ブooo〜ッ
VROOOM

SWOP
スポッ

キキッ
SKREECH

ガクン
SWING
ガクン
SWING

AH!
PITTER
PATTER

ARE WE NEAR THE MOUNTAINS ALREADY?
WE SURE ARE ROCKING A LOT.

I GUESS SEKI'S WEATHER CHARM WASN'T EFFECTIVE AFTER ALL.

NO WAY! THAT'S NOT FAIR!
WHAAT? IT'S STARTING TO RAIN!

IS UP-SIDE-DOWN!!
THE WEATHER DOLL

DON'T TELL ME THIS RAIN IS REALLY BECAUSE THAT DOLL IS UPSIDE-DOWN?
NO, IT COULDN'T HAVE SUCH AN OBVIOUS EFFECT...

MAKING THEM CHARMS FOR RAIN INSTEAD OF SUN-SHINE, RIGHT?
GOOD-WEATHER CHARMS UPSIDE-DOWN, IT REVERSES THEIR EFFECT
WHEN YOU TURN

NO, NO, EVERY-ONE'LL BE SO SAD!!
IF I LEAVE IT BE, WILL DOWN-POURS RUIN TODAY'S TOURS?

AND IT'S STUFFED WITH OTHER DOLLS, SO ITS NEGATIVE IMPACT COULD BE ESPE-CIALLY HUGE!
BUT THAT DOLL IS A SPECIAL ONE THAT SEKI WORKED HALF TO DEATH TO CREATE.

URGH ...
ZZZ...

SEKI!
ヒソ WHISPER WHISPER ヒソ
IT'S UPSIDE-DOWN!
FIX IT!

GOTO'S STILL FAST ASLEEP.
I GOTTA BE QUIET SO I DON'T WAKE HER.

FINE.
ギシッ
KREAK
I'LL FIX IT, THEN.
I GOTTA SAVE EVERY-ONE'S FUN FIELD TRIP!

そっ
REACH

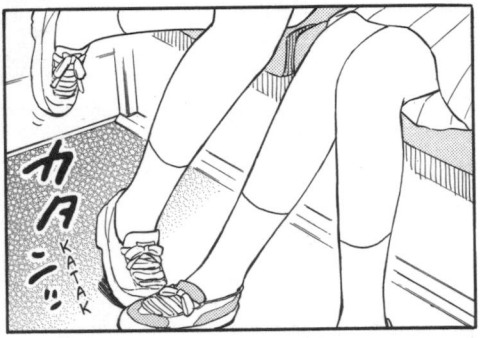
カタ
KATAK

IT'S STUCK...
HMM ...

OKAY.
HUH ?

THEY'RE BEING LOVEY-DOVEY AFTER ALL?!
I SNOOZE FOR A SEC, AND THIS HAPPENS?!

チラッ
GLANCE

BUT I THOUGHT YOKOI SAID SHE'D BE PATIENT WHILE ON THE BUS!
SURE, EVERYONE'S SLEEPING RIGHT NOW, SO THEY MIGHT NOT GET CAUGHT...

AH! ほっ
I SEE!

SO THEY'RE NOT MAKING OUT? THEN WHAT'S YOKOI DOING...
SEKI'S ASLEEP?!

ZZZ...

SHE'S GAZING AT HER BOY-FRIEND'S TOTALLY CUUUTE FACE, RIGHT?!
HIS SLEEP-ING FACE!

TUG
TUG
ぐいっ
ぐいっ
ALMOST, ALMOST THERE!

SNAP
ブツ

VERY WELL, I'LL FEIGN SLEEP TO SPARE HER HUMILIATION...
SHE TRIED TO BEHAVE, BUT THE LURE OF HIS SLEEPING FACE WAS TOO MUCH.

THE THREAD SNAPPED! WHAT NOW?!
FLAP
ばさっ
FLAP
ばさっ
HUH?!
WHAAT?!

EEE EEK!!
BURST
ばあっ

HOW FAR WILL YOU GO WITH A SLEEPING MAN?!
YOU'RE TOO WILD, YOKOI!

YOU'RE WAY TOO WORKED UP!!
A-ie
ギシッ
KREAK
ドタバタ
FLAIL
KREAK
ギシッ
FLAIL
ドタ
KREAK
ギシッ

WAAAH!
I GOTTA FIX IT BEFORE SEKI WAKES UP!

THIS MUST BE...
NO! THIS ISN'T THE YOKOI I KNOW!

ギュ PRESS
I'M WORRIED THAT THEIR RELATIONSHIP WILL BE EXPOSED DURING THE TRIP!
ウ
I CAN'T HELP: YOU KEEP IT QUIET ANY LONGER!!
ウウ

THIS SCHOOL TRIP HAS GOTTEN YOKO! ALL EXCITED!
HER FEELING LIBERATED!

HM? HUH?

SHFF
ササッ
WELL, THIS IS MY CHANCE!

RUSTLE
ごそごそ
RUSTLE

GOTO'S LEGS HAVE MOVED.
ISN'T SHE ASLEEP?

ふぅ〜っ
WHEW
DONE!
BUT MAYBE IT'S THANKS TO THAT WEATHER DOLL.
IT MUST BE COINCIDENCE,
THE RAIN HAS LET UP.
YAY!
I'M REALLY WORRIED!!
WILL IT FIT BACK IN?
SHOOVE
ギュウ
ウウ
I MISSED ONE!
TMBL
コロン
AH!

• 66th Period •

OUR GROUP IS HITTING BUSTLING TOURIST SIGHTS.
CHATTER
CHATTER
ワイ
ワイ
TODAY WE HAVE A FREE DAY.

FIELD TRIP, DAY 3.

AH.
THE BOYS ARE LAGGING BEHIND AGAIN.

RIGHT?
THIS IS YUMMY! I WANNA BUY MORE ON THE WAY BACK.

ばっ
WHIP
スチャッ
SNAP

GASP
RUSTLE
ゴソ
RUSTLE
ゴソ

JUST PRACTICING.
OH, NOTHING.
WHAT DID YOU SHOOT?

ぐび
GLUG
ぐび
GLUG
TSK.

I WANT TRAVEL PHOTOS OF THE ROBOT FAMILY!!

I HAVE A SECRET MISSION...
TO USE MY CAMERA TO TAKE PICS DURING THIS TRIP.

I HAVEN'T SEEN ANY SUSPICIOUS ACTIVITY SO FAR, BUT TODAY, WITH THIS FREE TIME, IS THE PERFECT CHANCE TO TAKE THEM OUT!
HE MADE MINI GUIDES FOR THEM, SO SEKI MUST'VE SNUCK THEM ALONG.
Trip Guidebook

I UNWITTINGLY TOOK THEM HOME BEFORE, BUT NOT THIS TIME!
INSTEAD I'LL TAKE HOME PHOTOS AS WELL AS MEMORIES.

S-SEKI TOURS ?!
TA-DAA
SEKI TOURS

HM?
WHAT'S THAT ON HIS BAG ...?

I'M SURE THEY'RE HERE.
BUT THERE'S BEEN NO SIGN OF THEM YET...

BUT HE'S JUST A STUDENT ON A FIELD TRIP!
SEKI TOURS
SO IS SEKI ACTING AS TOUR GUIDE, LEADING THE ROBOT FAMILY AROUND ?!

IS THAT A FLAG LIKE THE ONES TOUR GUIDES CARRY?

I WILL GET PHOTOS TO KEEP!
THE FAMILY MUST BE INSIDE HIS BAG!
BUT THAT MEANS THEY'RE THERE!

WE SHOULD VISIT THE SHRINE FIRST.
SO WHERE'S THE FIRST SHOP?

ざっ
SHUFFLE
SHUFFLE
ざっ

HAIYA!
JINGLE
JINGLE

I PRAY I CAN GET GOOD SHOTS!

パ
KLAP
パ
KLAP

HM?!

ぴたっ
FREEZE
Huh?
WHAT A UNIQUE PRAYER POSE...

ペコ
BOW
THEY'RE PRAYING!!

わたっ
FLAP
わたっ
FLAP
NO, WAIT, CAMERA, CAMERA!

PAYING RE-SPECTS AS A FAMILY!
HOW CHARM-ING!

ARGH!
SWIP
ひゅっ
RISE

I WASN'T MENTALLY PREPARED AT ALL!
THEY SHOWED UP SO SUD-DENLY!

LET ME TAKE A PHOTO!!
WAIT, WAIT, DON'T GO YET!!

SO, NEXT TIME!
BUT I KNOW NOW THEY'RE HERE.
パシャ
KASHIK

AH, OKAY.
SHOOT US!
RUMI, CAMERA!

OK!
THIS PLACE SHOULD BE HERE.
SHISHU

DON'T, THAT'S EMBARRASSING.
Power up!
I'M GONNA PAT IT ALL OVER!

UP YOUR HEALTH AND LUCK JUST BY TOUCHING IT!
Power
A POWER SPOT THAT'S POPULAR EVEN WITH THE LOCALS!
A 700-YEAR-OLD SACRED TREE!
700

OH, I'M JUST KIDDING! SORRY!
WHY SO PRICKLY?
DROOP しゅん
... SORRY.

DID HE GO OFF TO DO SOMETHING DURING THAT SHORT TIME?
SEKI WAS AWAY FROM THE GROUP.

HEY, SEKI, WHERE'VE YOU BEEN?

HUH? SURE.
I'M GOING ON AHEAD.
DASH ダッシュ

PING ピーン

キョロ
GLANCE
キョロ
GLANCE

HMM
?

THEY'RE HERE !!
ペっ
ナニ
CLING,

AND PLANS TO PICK THEM UP AFTER THEY'VE POWERED UP.
I SEE, HE PLACED THEM HERE AHEAD OF TIME

THE WHOLE FAMILY IS GIVING IT THEIR ALL! SO CUTE!
THEY'RE INCREASING THEIR LUCK AT THE POWER SPOT!

THAT VOICE...
Hm ?
HEY, IS THIS THAT POWER SPOT TREE?

NOW LET ME TAKE YOUR PICTURE !
HEH HEH HEH HEH
I CORRECTLY PREDICTED SEKI'S BEHAVIOR!

DON'T TOUCH IT, UZAWA!
THIS ROBOT IS WEARING A SWIMMING TUBE.
HA HA HA
OH, NO! UZAWA HAS PRIOR OFFENSES AGAINST THE ROBOT FAMILY!
I GOTTA PROTECT THEM...
IF HE FINDS THEM, HE MIGHT CARRY THEM OFF JUST FOR LAUGHS!

UZAWA!!
GIMME YOUR POWER!

...

ぺたーっ
CLING
...
HM?
AAARGH!
CHATTER
ワイワイ
HEY, LOOKIE! THIS IS FUNNY!
URGH!
プフッ
PFFT
IS THAT YOKOI? SHE'S TOO SERIOUS.
クス SNICKER
SHE MUST REALLY WANT SOME POWER.
クス SNICKER
UZAWA, YOU JERK!

HUNH ?!
BIGGLE
BIGGLE

RUMI ...
YOU'RE SUCH A HYPO-CRITE.
YOU JUST WANTED TO HOG THE POWER FOR YOURSELF.
NOOOOOO!
SHUDDER
GIT
SHUDDER

ALL RIGHT !
ME TOO, ME TOO!
Yaaay

HOW DARE YOU LAUGH AT ME, SEKI!!
GLARE
SHIVER
Whose fault do you think this is?!

BORING. I'M DONE.
THUP
THUP
I don't get it
THAT WAS FAST!

...

はっ
GASP

ふぅぅ
WHEEW
THE DANGER'S PAST FOR NOW.

RUMI, TAKE OUR PICTURE!
OH, SURE!

NOW, THEN.

パシャ
KASHAK
サッ
WHISK
サッ
WHISK

サ
RUSH
サ
RUSH
サッ
ピキ
PLINK

DROOOP
ぐてえ
えっ
HUH ...?
IS IT ALL IN OUR HEADS?

AHH, I FEEL ALL FULL OF POWER!
I FEEL SO SOOTHED.

女湯
Women's Baths

カポーン
SPLASH

MY FIELD TRIP IS OVER...
WHATEVER... WE'RE GOING HOME ON THE BUS TOMORROW.
YOU'RE SUCH A PAIN.

WILL YOU CHEER UP ALREADY, YOKO!?
I DUNNO WHAT YOUR DEAL IS.
BLUB
ブク
ブク
BLUB

NO WONDER MY SKIN FEELS SO SOFT.
HM ?
LIAR, YOU HAD NO IDEA.
Uh ha ha ha

HEY, IT SAYS THIS IS REAL HOT SPRING WATER!
HUH? OH, REALLY ?!

A REAL HOT SPRING ?!

男湯
Men's Baths
YOKO!?

ガヤ
ガヤ

HUH?

I JUST HAVE TO TAKE A PICTURE HERE!
WHAA?!

UM... WHAT'RE YOU DOING HERE?
AH, GOTO!
I'M WAITING FOR SEKI TO COME OUT!

HE WON'T HOLD BACK IF IT'S A REAL HOT SPRING.
I OUGHT TO BE ABLE TO CATCH 'EM ALL WARM FROM THE BATH.
HEH
HEH
HEH

SHE'S PLANNING TO SHOOT SEKI JUST OUT OF THE BATH!!
THE FAMILY

AT THIS RATE, THE PAIR'S SHAME-LESS ACTIONS WILL ATTRACT ATTEN-TION!!
YOKOI'S PATIENCE MUST HAVE REACHED ITS LIMIT!

EH HEH
MW EH HEH HEH
...

LEMME GO, LEMME GO!
YOU'VE GOT TO GO COOL OFF!
DRAG
ズル
DRAG
ズル
?

PLEASE FORGIVE ME!
ガッ
GRAB
HUH ?

YOU'D BETTER HURRY BEFORE IT'S TIME TO GO.
YOU HAVEN'T BOUGHT SOUVENIRS YET, YOKOI?
SHE'S WORSE THAN YESTERDAY.
UH, YEAH...

LAST DAY OF THE FIELD TRIP

HM ?!
SEKI ?

HAAH ...

WELL, YOU CAN'T BUY EVERYTHING YOU LIKE.
Hmm
IS THAT A WAY TO HAVE FUN... HM?

WHY DOES HE HAVE HIS CAMERA OUT?
IS HE SHOOTING SOUVENIRS?

WHAA AAAA ?!
KASHIK

MY LONG-AWAITED SHOT!
BUT I WANT A PIC, TOO!
SCHFF

DID HE MAKE ONE AT HOME FOR THE FAMILY?! THAT'S SILLY!
THEY ARE A STAPLE OF MANY TOURIST SITES, BUT...
IS THAT A PEEKA-BOO BOARD FOR SOU-VENIR PHOTOS ?!

HOME WITH ME!!
I'M TAKING THEM
I CAN'T SHOW MY LOVE FOR THE ROBOT FAMILY,
'CAUSE HE MIGHT FIGURE OUT I SNUCK THEM HOME LAST TIME.

SNIFF

JERK
URGH.

SNEAK

FIRST, I NEED TO ACT LIKE I'M NOT PAYING ATTENTION, THEN...
...

KASHIK

I DID IT!
I FINALLY GOT A TRAVEL PHOTO OF THE FAMILY!
PIP
DUCK

DASH

THE FIFTH TRIP ENDED IN DISAPPOINTMENT, AS SHE WAS UNABLE TO EVER GET A PICTURE.
WHAT'S WITH THAT STUPID PEACE SIGN?!
YOU'RE IN THE WAY!!
I WASN'T TAKING YOUR PIC SEKI!

PIP

Hmm

• 67th Period •
OF THIS TANKA POEM IS...
SO THE MEAN-ING

WHAT IS THAT FOR ...?
A TABLE ON TOP OF HIS DESK?

HM ?
TNK
ゴト

AH!
TWIRL
ヒュン

ARE THOSE MARBLES ?
ROLL
コロコロ
ROLL
ROLL
コロン

DID HE MAKE ALL THAT, INCLUDING THE TABLE?
NOW THAT IS A LITTLE MARVEL.

BILLIARDS
I DON'T KNOW THE RULES WELL, BUT...
I THINK YOU HIT NUMBERED BALLS WITH A WHITE ONE?

OOH!
VWOOOSH

OH, THERE'S THE WHITE ONE, THE CUE BALL!
THAT'S HOW HE'LL DEFEAT THE MON-STERS.
TMBL

I DON'T CARE ABOUT THE RULES, I WISH HE'D QUICKLY DROP THEM INTO THE POCKETS.
THEY'RE PAINTED WITH FACES, NOT NUMBERS! SCARY MONSTER FACES AT THAT...

IS HE REALLY CAPABLE OF KNOCKING DOWN THOSE MONSTERS ...?
I FEEL LIKE HE'S WAY SMALLER, TOO ...
ちょこっ
TMP
IT LOOKS LIKE AN ORDINARY PERSON.
WHOA, HOW PLAIN!
HE WAS REPELLED !!
THWAK
BOUNCE
BOUNCE
KTAK
I DON'T WANNA WATCH SOME JOHN DOE GET CHASED AROUND BY MONSTERS!
THAT'S NOT EVEN CLOSE TO A FIGHT!

MAYBE NOW THE MONSTERS CAN'T REPEL HIM?
HE PUT ON A MASK AND GOT BIGGER?

SKOP
カポッ
OOOOH?!

KRAK

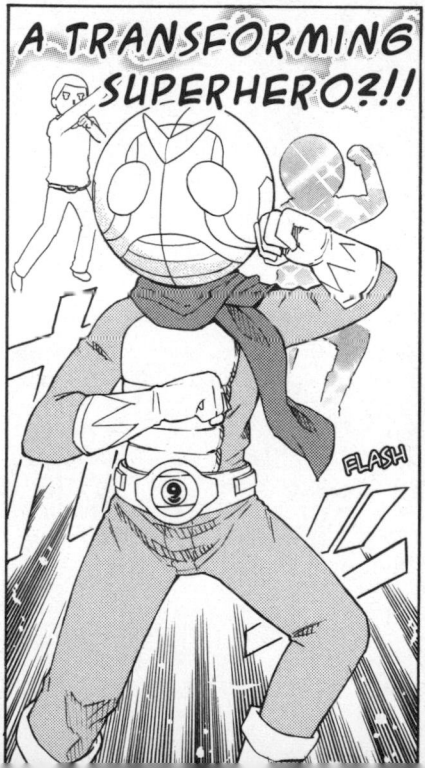
A TRANSFORMING SUPERHERO?!!
FLASH

KLUNK

IT BLEW AWAY ALL THE MONSTERS AT ONCE! COULD HE BE...
SO STRONG!
TNK
TNK
TNK
TNK

カ
KA
コツ
KLUNK
HM ?
AND I CAN WATCH THIS HERO IN ACTION WITHOUT WORRY!
I SEE! NOW HE CAN HANDLE THE MONSTERS, NO PROBLEM!
OKAY, THIS TIME.
コロ
ROLL
TOK
コツ
AH!
ROLL
コロ
THAT'S FUNNY.
I THOUGHT IT'D GONE IN THE HOLE...
IT WON'T GO IN?!
コテ
ツ
TMP
AH!
IF THE NUMBER OF MONSTERS NEVER DECREASES...
KLAK
カッ
TNK
コッ
KLIK
カ
TOK
コツ
OR WAIT, YOU DID THAT ON PURPOSE, DIDN'T YOU?!
YOU MESSED UP!
THE MONSTER IS BIGGER THAN THE HOLE!

THAT'S A DESPERATE BATTLE, EVEN FOR A HERO!
IT'LL ALWAYS BE NINE AGAINST ONE.

BUT THAT'S NO PROBLEM.
I'LL JUST ROUT THE MONSTERS INSTEAD!

トン
TAP

SEKI'S MOTIVE FROM THE GET-GO WAS TO WATCH THE HERO GET HURT.
WHAT A NASTY GAME THAT ONLY HE COULD THINK UP.

HUH?!
HEH
フッ

!

BUT THE HERO WOULD LOSE HIS POSITION!
SO I'D BECOME THE MAIN CHARACTER?!

WHY NOT? HE'S OKAY WITH ME BAILING OUT THE HERO?
HE DOESN'T RESENT ME INTERFERING?

IN THE HERO'S PLACE...?
ME, HELP? TAKE DOWN THE MONSTERS...

カッ
KTAK
TAK
カッ
カッ
TK
カッ
TK

I CAN ONLY SILENTLY CHEER HIM ON, NO MATTER HOW HARD THE BATTLE...
IF I DEFEAT THE MONSTERS, IT WOULDN'T BE HELPING HIM IN A REAL WAY.
GRIN
SLUMP
ガクッ

WAAH!
KRACK

HE'S BEEN DRIVEN INTO A CORNER!
IF THE MASK IS GONE, HE'LL BE SMALLER THAN THE MONSTERS AND HE WON'T BE ABLE TO FIGHT BACK!

HOW CAN SEKI LET THE HERO GET ALL BEATEN UP LIKE THAT?!
HE'S BEEN HIT SO MUCH HIS MASK CRACKED AND HIS PLAIN FACE IS SHOWING THROUGH!!

KLAK
カッ

NO, SEKI, STOP IT!!
KLAK
カン
TOK
ゴッ
BAM
ゴッ
KLAK
カン

NO, THOSE ARE...
WAS SEKI BEING CLUMSY?
TWO OF THE MON-STERS DROPPED OFF THE TABLE ?!
DNK
ゴッ
ROLL
コロ

!!
TOK
ゴッ
TNK
カッ

HIS UNFLAGGING HEART UNEXPECTEDLY CAME TO HIS AID!
THE TENACITY OF THE HERO WHO KEEPS FIGHTING EVEN WHEN HE'S IN TATTERS!

FRAGMENTS!
PIECES OF THE BROKEN MASK MESSED UP SEKI'S CALCULATIONS!

A HERO OF JUSTICE'S BATTLE !!
THIS IS TRUE METTLE !

SNAP
SNAP

HE'S INCORPORATING THE PIECES INTO HIS STRIKE STRATEGY ?!
NOD
NOD

* *Atsui*: Hot / Intense

68th Period

SPR
ピ
ン
ING
BUT I'D RATHER...

HE'S PULLING OUT SOME TOY AGAIN...
RUSTLE
ゴリ
RUSTLE
ゴリ

SKRITCH
かり
SKRITCH
かり

ぐしゅっ
SMAT
ぐしゅっ
SMAT

HE DO SOMETHING ABOUT
THAT CRAZY BEDHEAD FIRST.

THE TIME WHEN SEKI'S BAG COULD COME IN HANDY!
AH, THIS IS IT!
RUSTLE
ゴソ
RUSTLE
ゴソ

ピョーン
SPRING

HE'S GOT ALL THAT STUFF, BUT NOTHING TO FIX HIS BED-HEAD?!!
NOT!

HM?
カポッ
MAOA

GRAB
ガッ

BOYS... WHAT CAN YOU DO?
HE IS SO MULTI-TALENTED, EXCEPT WHEN IT COMES TO HIS APPEAR-ANCE.

RUSTLE
RUSTLE

HUH? WAAH!
そ〜っ
SHFF
HE'S GONNA TRY FIXING IT WITH GLUE?!

C'MON, A BRUSH IS NOTHING TO BE SURPRISED ABOUT.
IT SHOULD'VE BEEN THE FIRST THING TO COME TO MIND.
!
HERE, USE THIS!
TAK
コトロン
THEN WHAT DOES HE USE?
DOESN'T HE USUALLY USE A BRUSH?
BRUSH
サッ
BRUSH
サッ
そーっ
SFF
...
ピン
SPRING

WHAT?
WHY ARE YOU LOOKING AT ME WITH SUCH CONTEMPT ?!

LICK
ペロッ

YOU NEED TO USE WATER OR SOME-THING!
WHISPER
WHISPER
ヒソ
ヒソ
EVERY-ONE KNOWS THAT!

ゾクッ
SHIVER

WIPE
ふき
WIPE
ふき
...

I DIDN'T BRING ANY HAIR PROD-UCTS TODAY, EITHER ...
HMM
うーん
BUT IT LOOKS LIKE HE HAS NO WATER.

I SWEAR, BOYS ARE MISSING SOME-THING!
GEEZ, YOU CAN'T TREAT PEOPLE'S THINGS LIKE THAT!

HM ?
KLATTER
カラ
カラ
KLATTER

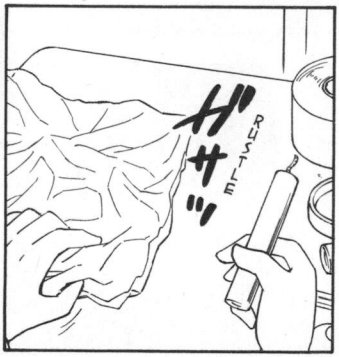
ガサ
RUSTLE

SIZZ
SIZZ
SIZZ
HE LIT A CANDLE ?!
DON'T PLAY WITH FIRE DURING CLASS!!
!!
BWOOSH
ボッ
A PLASTIC BAG?
ガサ
RUSTLE
ガサ
RUSTLE
HE PLACED THE BAG OVER THE CANDLE...
WHY ?
バサッ
FLAP
CINCH
ぎゅう
OH. GUESS HE GAVE UP ON FIXING HIS HAIR.
IS HE MAKING A HOT AIR BALLOON ?

10 MINUTES LATER.

IT'S COLD, SEKI!
SHIVER
ZWISH
ZWISH

WAIT, HE'S WRING-ING IT? WHY ...?
HE'S CRUSHING THE BAG ...?
SQUEEZE
SQUEEZE

THAT'S THAT BAG FROM EARLIER ?
RUSTLE
OH ?
RUSTLE

IS WATER ?!
COMING FROM INSIDE THAT EMPTY PLASTIC BAG...

?!
DRIP
DRIP
DRIP

UNBELIEVABLE, SEKI...
ACTUALLY GENERATED WATER IN THE MIDDLE OF CLASS!!

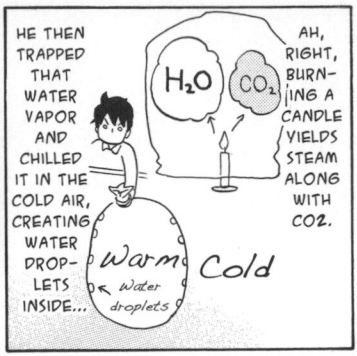
AH, RIGHT, BURNING A CANDLE YIELDS STEAM ALONG WITH CO2.
H2O
CO2
HE THEN TRAPPED THAT WATER VAPOR AND CHILLED IT IN THE COLD AIR, CREATING WATER DROPLETS INSIDE...
Warm
Cold
Water droplets

HE USED THE FACT THAT THE WATER VAPOR VOLUME IN AIR CHANGES AT DIFFERENT TEMPERATURES.
Warm
Steam
Steam
Steam
WE LEARNED THIS IN SCIENCE CLASS...
Cold
Steam
Uhm uhm

BRUSH
BRUSH

AND WE'RE CURRENTLY IN LANGUAGE CLASS.
HE USUALLY DOESN'T STUDY A BIT, BUT HE USES HIS BRAIN AT TIMES LIKE THESE.
SPLATCH

Continued in My Neighbor Seki Volume 6

Fresh Vegetables & Fruits Tai
ISN'T THAT...
AH!
BONUS ①
HOW ADMI-RABLE!
IS SHE RUNNING ERRANDS ?
SEKI'S LITTLE SISTER, JUN !!
Sigh
SWFF
SWFF
SHAKE
SHAKE
SWFF
SWFF

HOW MATURE!
Or is that to be expected?
HAGGLING OVER PRICES?
SHE'S DOING SOME HIGH-LEVEL TRANSACTION!!
NOW SCRAM, YA THIEF!!
AS ALWAYS, I'M NO MATCH FOR YOU, MISS.

COULD THEY BE FOR SEKI?
AH!

WHY IN THE WORLD...
BUT THOSE ARE BIG. ARE THEY MEN'S?
...
She's waffling

SHE'S LOOKING AT GLOVES?
OH, AN ACCESSORY SHOP NEXT?

SHE REALLY LOVES HER BROTHER, HUH.
WHAT AN AMAZING GIRL!

OH!
はっ
GLOVES!!

MAYBE SHE'S SAVED UP MONEY SAVED BY HAGGLING?
A GIFT FOR HER BIG BRO!

AND I'LL GET TO SPEND A LOVELY FEW DAYS WITH JUN ALL TO MY-SELF!
WE CAN HAVE A FRIENDLY KNITTING CLASS !!

JUN SEEMS FAIRLY HANDY, AND IF I (A 2ND RANK KNITTING LICENSEE) TEACH HER...
IF THEY'RE A GIFT, SHE SHOULD KNIT HIM A PAIR HERSELF!

IF I CAN TEACH HER...
THAT'S RIGHT!

TIP
TOE
SALE SALE
MUST MAKE IT SEEM LIKE PURE CHANCE.

LET'S PITCH IT TO JUN!
キャーッ
WHEE!
YES, YES, LEAVE IT TO ME!
SCAMPER
SCAMPER

MAYBE I'LL GO KNIT A PAIR AT HOME. I'VE GOT SO MUCH YARN!
AHH あー
YEAH, HAND-MADE IS THE BEST!

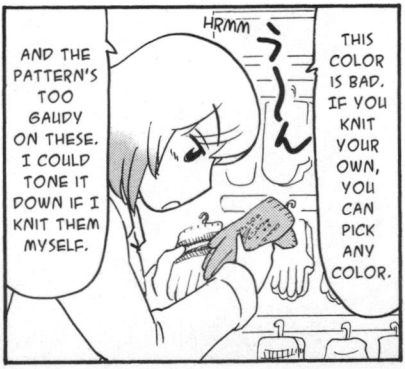
AND THE PATTERN'S TOO GAUDY ON THESE. I COULD TONE IT DOWN IF I KNIT THEM MYSELF.
HRMM うーん
THIS COLOR IS BAD. IF YOU KNIT YOUR OWN, YOU CAN PICK ANY COLOR.

そおーっ
PEEK
HUH? SHE'S GONE ?!
EXCUSE ME, MISS.
ビクッ
JOLT

AAARGH!
I DON'T CARE WHETHER YOU BUY OR NOT,
BUT DON'T SCARE OFF CUSTOMERS.
I'M SO SORRY, I'M SO SORRY!!

SOME DAYS LATER.
AWW
STAARE
じと〜っ
MY ONE CHANCE ...
?

THANKS TO ALL YOUR SUPPORT, THERE'S BEEN A BIG DEVELOPMENT... MY NEIGHBOR SEKI IS BEING ADAPTED INTO AN ANIME.
THUS, A LOT HAS BEEN GOING ON, BUT IF I TOLD YOU, THAT WOULD SPOIL IT, SO I CAN'T SAY ANY-THING.
IT'S A SEKI TRAIT I'M AFRAID (BEING A SERIES OF ONE-SHOTS).
BONUS 2
THANK YOU SO MUCH FOR READING MY NEIGHBOR SEKI VOLUME 5.
I'D BE SO GLAD IF YOU ENJOYED IT.

SO I TRY TO PRESENT A CHEERFUL FACE TO THE CAMERA, BUT...
パシャ KASHIK
I WANT TO BE SEEN AS A GOOD PERSON BY THOSE LOOKING AT MY PICTURE,
KASHIK パシャッ

SINCE I DON'T CARE TO CREATE A MYSTERIOUS AURA, I SHOW MY FACE.
AND PHOTO SHOOTS, OF COURSE.
AS THE ANIME PRODUCTION PROGRESSED, I, AS THE CREATOR, HAVE HAD MANY INTERVIEWS

NOW SMILE, PLEASE!
BIG SMILE, SMILE!
UH, I THOUGHT I WAS SMILING, SO WHY DOESN'T IT LOOK LIKE I AM?!

IF YOU WANT ME TO SMILE, DO SOMETHING TO MAKE ME CRACK ONE! OR ELSE JUST SAY, "A FAKE SMILE IS JUST FINE," OKAY?
I'm not an actor, you know!
They don't spontaneously generate!
IT'S NOT POSSIBLE TO CREATE A "NATURAL SMILE" WHEN THERE'S NOTHING TO LAUGH AT!
I'M NOT GOOD AT MANUFACTURING SMILES FOR PICTURES...
AND I DO SMILE, NORMALLY, TOO, BUT...

IF YOU WORE NICE CLOTHES, YOU'D LOOK SO MUCH BETTER!
She's super-nice, so her words felt extra harsh
...
WHY AREN'T YOU DRESSED UP?
EXAMPLE OF SOMETHING THAT CAME AS A SHOCK (1): ONCE, LONG AGO, I WORKED HARD TO DRESS UP FOR A PUBLISHER'S PARTY, WHEN A MENTOR SAID:

I'VE HAD SIMILAR EXPERIENCES.
Just a mini-shock!
WELL, I'M NOT ACTUALLY THAT MAD ABOUT IT.
I'll forget by morning!

LIPSIE よいしょ
LET'S SLEEP, LET'S SLEEP.
AH, I WANT TO FORGET IT.

PLEASE WATCH THE ANIME!
Check it out online!
WELL, SEE YOU NEXT VOLUME!

I talked back this time
I DID SHAVE!
HA! HA! HA!
THIS IS THE BEST I CAN DO!
HEY MAN, WILL YOU AT LEAST SHAVE?
EXAMPLE OF SOMETHING THAT CAME AS A SHOCK (2): A DRINKING PARTY AT A NEARBY FRIEND'S HOME. I'D CHECKED MYSELF OVER BEFORE LEAVING MY HOUSE, BUT...